0\20

CHRISTIAN LIGHT EDUCATION
Reading Series

Doors to Discovery

Third Grade Reader

Compiled by Ruth K. Hobbs

CHRISTIAN LIGHT EDUCATION
A division of **Christian Light Publications**
Harrisonburg, Virginia 22802   (540) 434-0750   www.clp.org/cle

CHRISTIAN LIGHT
Reading Series

DOORS TO DISCOVERY
Christian Light Education, a division of
Christian Light Publications, Inc., Harrisonburg, VA 22802
© 2000 by Christian Light Publications, Inc.
All Rights Reserved.
Printed in China

Sixth Printing, 2014

ISBN: 978-0-87813-937-8

Table *of* Contents

307

308

Doors to Discovery

"Teacher," I said, "I want to know
About *everything!* How airplanes work
   And why the sun goes down at night—
   Where does it go? Do the stars give light
In the day? And where do lions and tigers live?
   And how fast—*really*—can antelopes run?
   Is there such a thing as a midnight sun?"

   "What a lot of questions!" my teacher cried.
   "I haven't time to answer them all.
      But here is a chair in a quiet nook,
      And near it a shelf with many a book.
   Just pull one down and begin to read;
      You'll learn a lot if you start to look
      Through the pages of an open book."

So now I know the secret of books—
They are ships and wings to far-off lands;
They are winding roads; they are worlds to explore;
They are open doors to discover more.

—Jennifer Crider

"Let us walk honestly."

– Romans 13:13

Too Honest

"The trouble with you," said Jack, "is that you're too honest for your own good, Kenny. You had just as many baskets of cherries as I had last year. If you had filled them the way I filled mine, you would have made as much money as I did."

Kenny watched as Jack filled his baskets—little cherries on the bottom, big ones on the top.

"Yes, I guess I should have done it your way," he said, "but it didn't seem quite honest. No one wanted to buy my baskets of little cherries even at a lower

price. I ended up giving them to Aunt May. She made jelly with them."

"See, that's what I'm saying," said Jack. "You are too honest for your own good. Look at all the money you lost. You didn't even sell your little ones. You can sell them all if people think the whole basket is filled with big cherries. You don't have to say they are all big. Just don't say anything. They will go away happy. You never see them again, anyway."

As he walked back to his uncle's farm, Kenny thought about what Jack had said. When he reached his cherry tree, he stood there looking at it for a while.

He remembered how happy he had been when his uncle had given him this one tree for his own and said he could have his own roadside stand. But he remembered the rest too. After all the trouble he had taken to sort out his cherries, nobody bought the little ones when the baskets of big ones were gone.

"I suppose Jack is right," he said to himself. "It would be better to put the little cherries on the bottom, as long as I don't say they are all big. That way I won't have any cherries left over and will get a good price for every basket. It takes me just as long to pick little cherries as big ones."

The next day Kenny started to pick his cherries. He worked alone, so it took two days to do all the picking.

Then it took several hours to put them into the baskets. He did it just as Jack said—little ones on the bottom, big ones on the top. But he wasn't whistling as he usually did, because somehow, he didn't feel so good about what he was doing.

When Kenny had finished filling the last basket, it was time for dinner.

"Well," said Aunt May, as Kenny came into the house, "I hope you'll sell all your cherries this year."

"So do I," said Kenny. "Jack opened his stand yesterday. He said he's selling to lots of strangers this year."

"I'm not surprised," said Aunt May. "I'm sure the people who bought from him last year wouldn't come back for more this year."

Kenny looked at Aunt May in surprise. "What do you mean, Aunt May?" he asked.

"You told me yourself how he fills his baskets," said Aunt May. "He makes people think they are getting big cherries when the baskets are half full of little ones. Who would come back for more of that kind of cherries?"

"But Jack says a lot of people do that," said Kenny.

"If a lot of people do something wrong, does it start being right?" asked Aunt May.

Kenny wasn't listening to her anymore, for something behind her had caught his eye. There in the cupboard were the jars of cherry jelly that Aunt May had made from his leftover cherries last year.

"That's the reward I got for being so honest," he said to himself. "Jack was right. I was too honest for my own good. I'll come out better this year since I sorted my cherries the way he did."

The next morning, Kenny had just put out all his baskets of cherries when the first car stopped in front of his stand. The lady in the car waved to Kenny to come to her window.

"Hello," she said. "How are the cherries this year?"

"Fine," said Kenny. "Would you like a basket or two this morning?"

"I hope they are as good as they were last year," said the lady. "When I got home, I wished I had bought more."

Kenny could feel his face getting red as the lady talked on. "I came back for more the next day," she said, "but your stand was closed. So I bought two baskets from that other boy down the road. My, what a difference! Never again!"

Kenny did not know what to say, so he didn't say anything. But the lady went right on talking. "Well, I'm in a hurry this morning. I don't have to get out to look at your cherries. I know they will be good. Bring me two baskets, please."

Kenny hurried back to the stand. He poured all the cherries out of two of the baskets, hoping that the lady couldn't see what he was doing. Then he quickly filled them with big cherries off the tops of other baskets.

The lady looked very pleased when he handed her the baskets through the window. "My! What beautiful cherries," she said, as she paid him.

As soon as she had gone, Kenny poured the cherries out of all the baskets. He started sorting them over again—big cherries in these baskets, little ones in those. He would have to make new price signs, but that wouldn't take long. Suddenly he started whistling.

A little while later, Kenny was still busy sorting the cherries when he heard footsteps. Aunt May was coming with a big box in her arms.

"Why, Kenny," she said. "I thought you had finished filling your baskets yesterday."

"I thought so too," said Kenny, "but I just realized that I hadn't done a very good job, so I'm doing it over."

"I see," said Aunt May. "Well, here, Kenny, I brought you a surprise. These are the jars of jelly that I made out of your leftover cherries last year. They are yours to sell. The money you get from them will be more than what you would have gotten for the little cherries, even if you had sold them."

Kenny stared in surprise at the jars of jelly his aunt was setting out on the stand. "Oh, Aunt May!" he cried at last. "Thank you! Thank you! You are wonderful!"

7

Aunt May smiled. "I think you are pretty special too, Kenny," she said. "And I hope you'll always remember something: It is never too late to start doing what you should have done all along."

Kenny watched Aunt May walk back to the house. "I wonder," he said to himself, "I wonder if she knew."

– Marion Mitchelson Gartler

*"Thine, O Lᴏʀᴅ, is the greatness . . . for all
that is in the heaven and in the earth is thine."*

– 1 Chronicles 29:11

Adventure After Dark

One spring afternoon, Dick asked his father, "May I
go down to the pond with Jim tonight? He wants to use
his big new flashlight and watch the frogs puff out their
necks and sing."

"May I go too? I want to go too," said Nancy.

"Oh, you would be afraid," said Dick. "You are only
six, and you always yell
when something
scares you."

"Now, Dick,
Nancy will never
learn not to be
afraid of things
until you take her
along and tell her
about them," said
Father. "You may

9

go with Jim, but Nancy may go too.

"And Nancy, you must be quiet and not yell if something makes you afraid. You will not see much if you don't keep quiet."

Dick and Nancy could hardly wait for the last light of day to **fade** away. At last darkness fell, and Dick's friend Jim came up from his house with his big flashlight.

Nancy held fast to Dick's hand as they went down across the barnyard to the pond. Jim's flashlight shone ahead of them. Things looked strange at night—not at all as they did in the daytime.

Suddenly Nancy stopped and cried, "Oh-h-h-h! Look! There is something in that tree! Take me back! I want to go back to the house!"

Dick covered Nancy's mouth with his hand. "Be quiet," he said. "I knew it would be this way. I knew you would be afraid. We cannot go back now. You will just have to go along and try not to be frightened. And you must keep quiet or we will not see anything."

But even Dick and Jim were frightened when they saw what Nancy pointed at—two great eyes shining in the full light of the flashlight.

One moment they saw the eyes. The next moment they didn't. Then the children heard a call, *Whoo-oo whoo-whoo-whoo,* and a big bird flew silently into the air and away.

"Just an owl," whispered Dick, and they all laughed

at themselves for being afraid of an owl.

While Dick helped Nancy climb the stone wall, they heard a little noise near them. Jim pointed the light into the wall. There they saw two shining little eyes looking at them from a hole in the rocks.

"What is it?" asked Nancy softly.

"A mouse. Probably a white-footed mouse," said Jim in a low tone. "It is a good thing we came along. Maybe that owl wanted it for his supper. We saved its life. It might have been eaten in another moment."

Nancy stepped quietly down on the other side of the wall and tried not to be afraid anymore. "We should come here and save something's life every night," she said.

The songs from the pond grew louder. "There must be hundreds of them," whispered Dick. "Are they all frogs? What is that strange **trilling** sound?"

"Toads make that trilling sound," said Jim. "It is tiny frogs called spring peepers that do all that peeping—like baby chicks. And the croaking comes from bigger frogs."

Now all this time their old friend, Hoppy Hoptoad, had been singing with the other frogs and toads. Hoppy lived under the front porch steps of their house. He had hopped down to the pond as soon as the other toads and the frogs had begun singing.

Hoppy saw the flashlight coming down the path, but he was not frightened by the children. He kept trilling with all his might.

Hoppy did not hear the strange sound in the grass. He did not see the strange, long something that slid up to him.

Suddenly Hoppy could not see the children's light. He could not breathe. He could not hear. He could not sing. Something had covered his head. Up he went into the air.

Just at that moment Jim pointed the flashlight at the ground, and Nancy yelled out so loudly that the two boys jumped. Then they looked where she pointed, and there in the shining light they saw a strange-looking something.

"Oh, it is just a snake," said Jim. "That kind won't hurt you."

"Look at the legs and arms growing out of its mouth!" cried Nancy. "I never saw a snake like that!"

"She is right, Jim," cried Dick. "Look at it!"

Jim looked. Then he said, "Watch." He put his hand around the snake near its head. Out of the snake's mouth fell a toad.

At last Hoppy could breathe. At last he could see. At last he was on the ground again. With one big hop he disappeared down the path toward the pond.

"It was a toad!" cried Nancy.

"Oh, good, we have saved another life," said Dick. "But take that snake away, Jim."

Jim put the snake down and made it go the other way into the grass.

Then Nancy said, "Why is everything so quiet? The toads and frogs are not singing."

"We have made too much noise," said Jim. "Now we will just have to stand still and wait. Maybe they will begin to sing again."

Jim turned off the flashlight and they waited in the darkness. Soon one frog started to croak. Then the spring peepers began. Before long hundreds of frogs were singing again.

The children moved slowly and quietly to the dark pond. Jim turned on the flashlight. There they saw frogs with their necks puffed out, singing away. Some were little green frogs. Some were old grandfather bullfrogs.

Suddenly Nancy saw something beside her shoe. She looked closer. There sat a big toad, trilling away.

"Look at this toad," she said softly. "He is singing like

a frog. I didn't know toads could sing like that."

"Pick it up, Nancy," said Jim.

"No, indeed," Nancy said. "I don't want to get **warts**."

"You won't get warts. Toads can't give you warts. That is just an old, made-up story. Those bumps have a bad taste. A cat or dog or fox tries to eat a toad only one time."

"I'll pick it up," said Dick, and he lifted the toad very carefully. The toad was not frightened in Dick's hand.

"Maybe it is Hoppy Hoptoad," said Nancy. "It looks like Hoppy. Maybe he has come down from the house to sing with the other toads and the frogs."

"Oh, all toads look alike," said Jim. "This toad can't be Hoppy."

But Jim was not right about that. The toad in Dick's hand was indeed their old friend, Hoppy Hoptoad.

Hoppy had forgotten all about being frightened. He had forgotten what had happened to him just a few minutes ago. All he knew was that it was spring and that he was not afraid of anything. He could see and he could hear and he could sing.

As the children went back through the darkness to the house, Nancy did not hold Dick's hand. She had learned that the darkness is full of many things you cannot see in the daylight. And there is nothing to be afraid of, nothing at all.

—adapted

A Song for Twilight

In all the folds of heaven, the stars
   Are still as huddled sheep.
The tired birds, their songs all said,
   In treetops are asleep.

A slow wind walks the quiet world
   With little steps and light,
And sings a drowsy lullaby—
   Good-night, good-night, good-night.

– Nancy Byrd Turner

> *"Thou makest darkness, and it is night:*
> *wherein all the beasts of the forest do creep forth."*
>
> – Psalm 104:20

Danger in the Cornfield

Mrs. Raccoon and her twins had come a long, long way from home. For three nights they had walked. During the day they had slept in many different nests along the way. Ricky and Racky had been surprised to learn that the family had more than one nest.

Now they **scampered** happily along in the darkness with their mother. They felt they were near the end of their trip, for the trees were thinning out. Suddenly they came out on a quiet, dark hilltop where they could look out over the countryside.

The twins did not know why they had come so far from home, but their mother knew what she was doing. There was danger in this adventure, but she had determined to get some milky white corn. Of all the many things raccoons eat, nothing tastes so delicious as fresh corn on the cob. So a farmer's cornfield is a wonderful place to spend a night. That is why Mother Raccoon had traveled so far from home.

Ricky and Racky could not see the farmhouse or the barn standing on the other side of the field of corn.

Mrs. Raccoon could not see them either, but she knew they were there. She knew, too, that houses and barns and fields of corn meant other things—things like dogs and men and guns.

So now Mrs. Raccoon moved along very quietly toward the cornfield. She stayed close to the stone walls, climbing over those in their path. Slowly they neared the cornfield. Ricky and Racky began to smell something wonderful. They eagerly followed their mother toward that smell. At last the tall stalks stretched above them. They had reached the cornfield.

Mrs. Raccoon began to climb a stalk as she would climb a tree. Soon the stalk could bear her weight no longer. It fell over. Their mother fell with it, but she was not hurt, for it was not far to the ground. Then she pulled back the green husks from an ear of corn, and Ricky and Racky dug their little teeth into the milky white corn. Never had they eaten anything so delicious. They ate all around the ears, from end to end.

The twins soon learned to husk the corn themselves. Sometimes when they pulled back the husks and took a bite or two, they found that the corn was not ripe. Then they went on to another ear. In that way they spoiled more ears than they ate.

Dozens of cornstalks soon lay flat on the ground, with their ears torn open and chewed on.

The three raccoons stayed in the field until the blackness of night began to fade into gray. Morning was coming, so Mrs. Raccoon headed for the woods. The little ones, full of corn, slowly **waddled** after her.

As Racky climbed over the stone wall, a stone rolled loose and rattled to the ground.

Suddenly a dog barked. The farmer's dog had heard the rolling stone.

Mrs. Raccoon began to run so fast that the twins could hardly keep up with her. For the first time in their lives Ricky and Racky knew the meaning of **terror**.

At the edge of the cornfield, the dog picked up their trail. His bark became more eager and excited as he got nearer and nearer. There was only one thing for Mrs. Raccoon to do. She led the way to a tree and pushed the twins up the trunk. They scrambled in terror up into the branches of the big oak. When they were safely out of sight, the mother ran a little way from the tree to throw the dog off the trail of her babies.

Then she turned to face the dog as it ran into the open not far from where she stood. The dog stopped in his tracks. Then he circled and tried to get behind her. Mrs. Raccoon kept turning to face him as he ran around looking for a chance to jump in and grab her. Her wide-open mouth showed sharp white teeth.

Up in the tree, Ricky and Racky trembled with terror. They wanted Mother. Suddenly Racky did a very foolish thing. He scrambled down the tree and ran toward his mother.

Quickly the dog turned and jumped for the baby raccoon. But he had not counted on Mrs. Raccoon. With her green eyes shining and her fur standing up, she fell upon the dog and sank her sharp teeth into his nose. With a loud **yelp**, he backed away and shook off the angry mother. Then, yelping at every jump, he fled back the way he had come.

The minute Mrs. Raccoon was sure the dog had gone for good, she turned to Racky and nosed him softly. She looked over his fur coat to see if he was hurt. Except for a scratch on one of his ears, Racky was fine. Then she smoothed down her own beautiful fur.

Ricky came scrambling down the tree and ran to his mother and brother, touching each of them with his little black nose to make sure they were all right.

They must waste no time. For all Mrs. Raccoon knew, the man who carried a gun had followed the dog. She could fight a dog, but she could not fight a man with a gun.

Chirring softly, she turned and headed into the woods. If she could find a creek, she would travel some distance in the water to throw the dog off their trail. The important thing now was to hurry.

Ricky and Racky scrambled after their mother as fast as their short little legs could go. On and on they went. Now and then Mrs. Raccoon turned and looked behind them and listened for a moment, but all seemed quiet. All three of them would be glad to get back to the safe, cozy hollow in their home tree, far from the danger in the cornfield.

−Jane Tompkins

At Dusk
the Wild Creatures Move

At dusk,
When the sun falls over the rim of the world—
Then the deer feeds at the forest's edge.

At dusk,
When bits of gray light still linger—
Then the fox roams the ridges in search of food.

At dusk,
When shadows gather and darkness spreads—
Then the bat tumbles through the night air.

At dusk,
When stars open their sharp silver eyes—
Then the whippoorwill clamors from deep in the woods.

At dusk,
When the moon waxes bright in the sky—
Then the raccoon visits the farmer's cornfield.

At dusk,
When the night-black dark deepens—
Then the owl hoots and all little things tremble.

At dusk,
In the safety of twilight—
Then the wild creatures move.

—Jennifer Crider

> *"That they which have believed in God might
> be careful to maintain good works."*
>
> – Titus 3:8

I Don't Care

"James, you are wasting your time playing with that
kitten when you ought to be doing your homework," said
Mother Mason. "You will get bad grades if you don't have
your **assignments** done."

"I don't care," replied the boy as he continued to
amuse his pet with a spool tied to a string.

"But you ought to care, dear," said Mother seriously.
"You will grow up to be an **ignorant**, useless man if you
do not learn to make good use of your time."

"I don't care. It is no fun doing things you *have* to
do all the time. I won't be a man for ages and ages.
And I don't care if I am ignorant. Anyway, I'll get to
my assignments right after supper." And with his kitten
over his arm, James ran out the door.

His mother had noticed that lately James replied to

so many things with, "I don't care." At first she thought he was copying a saying from the big boys at school. If so, it now was a habit with him.

"'I don't care' will be the ruin of James," said Mrs. Mason to her husband when he came home from work a short while later. "Do you have any good ideas how we might help him?"

Mother and Father talked together for quite a while, sometimes smiling, sometimes looking serious. But in the end they agreed on a plan that they hoped would help James see the evil in the habit he had picked up.

The Masons lived near the school and James always came home for lunch. The next day he came rushing in at noon as usual.

He stopped short. The table was not set. Mother sat in her rocking chair, mending. James had never seen his mother sewing at lunchtime.

"Mother, it's lunchtime. I need to eat."

"I don't care," said Mother, without looking up.

"But I'm hungry," said James.

"I don't care," repeated his mother.

James stared at her. Mother had never talked to him like that before. Never in his life had he heard her say, "I don't care."

He stood silent a while, and then his face grew red as he suddenly remembered what he and his mother had talked about the evening before.

What could he do? Finally he said, "Mother, I really
am terribly hungry. I'm nearly starved."

"I don't care," she said again.

"But the noon recess will soon be over. I won't get back in time. I must finish an assignment before school starts again. I might even be late for class."

"I told you, James, I don't care," said Mother again. "Since you don't mind being ignorant, it doesn't matter if you get back late. It doesn't matter if you finish the assignment or not." And his mother went on with her sewing.

This was too much for the boy. What if his mother really never did anything for him anymore! How would he ever get along if his mother didn't care for him? He burst into tears.

Mother, seeing him serious at last, laid down her sewing and called him to her side. She put her arm around him and said, "James, Father and I want to make you see how wrong it is to say, 'I don't care.' Suppose we really did not care for you. What would you do for meals and clothes and a nice home?

"You see we must care for you, or you will **suffer** very seriously. We must care even when it calls for work we do not enjoy.

"You suffered when I didn't care about whether or not you had lunch. Don't you think others suffer when you don't care about doing the things you ought?

"Think of your schoolteacher. He spends many hours preparing lessons to help you learn the things every boy must know. Think how selfish and **ungrateful** you sound when you say, 'I don't care whether I do my assignments or not.'

"More than that, our heavenly Father cares for us all the time. What would you do if He said, 'I don't care about James Mason'?

"Father and I want you to stop saying 'I don't care.' We want you to work hard to be a thoughtful, thankful boy who does care about others. We don't want an ignorant boy. We want a boy who does what he should do without grumbling. Only then will you be happy. Only then can you please our heavenly Father who cares for us."

James had never thought of his careless habit in this way before. He dried his tears and, after eating a quick lunch, went **soberly** back to school.

–adapted

> *"A soft answer turneth away wrath."*
>
> – Proverbs 15:1

Couldn't Aggravate Me

Frank Benson came home from school one day with a troubled look on his face.

"Well, Frank," said Daddy, "what happened today that makes you look so glum? Wasn't your homework done right?"

"My lessons aren't difficult," said Frank. "But some of the big boys **pester** me, so that I almost hate to go to school."

"Pester you, Frank? What do they find to tease you about?"

"Oh, they call me 'Baby Benson' and '**cunning** little Frank,' and they make fun of my coat because the sleeves are a little too short. Today after school Sam and Will kept saying, 'What a good little baby he is!' and 'How can such a little head carry so much learning?' It makes me almost **dread** to answer in class or have my work done right.

"Of course they do it when the teacher isn't around, but I know if I told on them they would pester me all the more."

"I am sure of that," said Daddy. "But that shouldn't be such a difficult problem. Why do you *let* them **aggravate** you? No one can aggravate you if you refuse to be aggravated."

"I can't help what they do, Daddy. I wouldn't get aggravated if they didn't talk like that. They think it is the greatest fun and keep it up all the more when they see that I get aggravated.

"I have asked them nicely to stop. I have acted like I didn't care. I have pretended I didn't hear them. And, of course, sometimes I have gotten cross and said ugly things back to them."

"I can tell you how to take all the fun out of it for them," said Daddy.

"It is no use, Daddy. I have tried every way I can think of, but those big boys are so mean that nothing will change them. School wouldn't be fun for them if they couldn't pester me or someone else."

"I know of a way you haven't tried, Frank. That is the Bible way. You know the Bible says, 'A soft answer turneth away **wrath**.' That means to talk quietly. I think it also means not to use hard words that hurt others. Soft words turn away the anger of others. A soft answer turns away your own anger too.

"If those big boys see that you aren't the least bit aggravated by their mean teasing, it won't be fun for them any more.

"Try the Bible way tomorrow. Meet those boys with a cheerful face and a pleasant word. If they begin their old game, join with them in the fun. Laugh with them when they laugh at you. No matter what they say, just refuse to let it aggravate you. You will see their teasing will stop after a while. It will be difficult, but just give it a try."

"But what should I say?"

"Just agree with them. If they make fun of how short you are, say you know you are little and hope you will grow as big as they someday. If they make fun of your coat, stick your arms out further yet, to show how short your sleeves really are. If you make a mistake, be the first one to laugh and say, 'Now wasn't that silly of me,' or something like that. Don't ever be too proud to laugh at yourself."

"Well, I have never tried talking like that," said Frank slowly. "I'll give it a try tomorrow. But I still think they are to blame for making me aggravated."

⁊   ⁊   ⁊   ⁊   ⁊

The next afternoon Frank came running from school with a happy face. "It worked, Daddy. It worked great. No one aggravated me all day long. I tried it on

Sam and Will and pretty soon they left me alone, and now I like school again."

"Did you think the Bible way wouldn't work?" asked Daddy with a smile.

"No, I didn't think that, only I had never tried out that verse before. But now I know a soft answer really does turn away wrath. It was a funny thing, but when I tried to think of something kind or jolly or pleasant to say, somehow I didn't feel cross anymore.

"It worked just like you said; they couldn't aggravate me because I refused to get aggravated," finished Frank with a satisfied nod of his head. "Now I know how to handle those big boys."

–adapted

> *"And he put them all out, and took her by the*
> *hand, and called, saying, Maid, arise."*
>
> – Luke 8:54

Come Back, Little Girl

41. And, behold, there came a man named Jairus, and he was a ruler of the **synagogue**: and he fell down at Jesus' feet, and besought him that he would come into his house:

42. For he had one only daughter, about twelve years of age, and she lay a dying. But as he went the people thronged him.

49. While he yet spake, there cometh one from the ruler of the synagogue's house, saying to him, Thy daughter is dead; trouble not the Master.

50. But when Jesus heard it, he answered him, saying, Fear not: believe only, and she shall be made whole.

51. And when he came into the house, he suffered no man to go in, save Peter, and James, and John, and the father and the mother of the maiden.

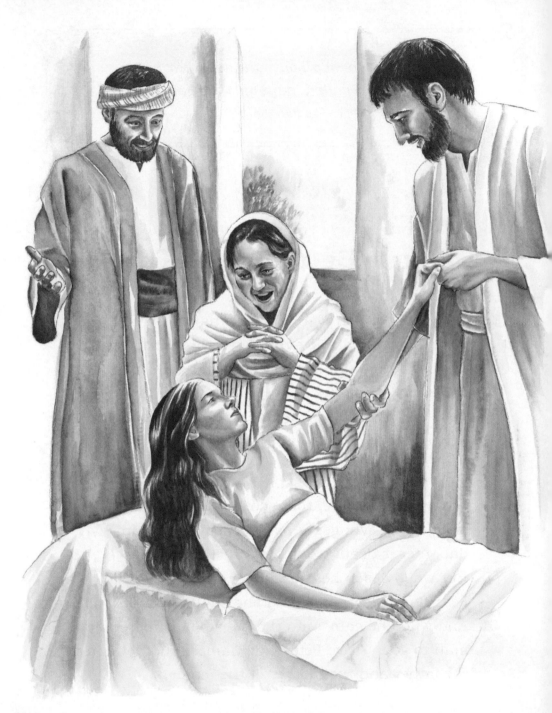

52. And all wept, and bewailed her: but he said, Weep not; she is not dead, but sleepeth.
53. And they laughed him to **scorn**, knowing that she was dead.
54. And he put them all out, and took her by the hand, and called, saying, Maid, arise.
55. And her spirit came again, and she arose straightway: and he commanded to give her meat.
56. And her parents were **astonished**: but he charged them that they should tell no man what was done.

–Luke 8:41, 42, 49-56

"Be not overcome of evil, but overcome evil with good."

– Romans 12:21

The Dreadful Paul

"Mama, why is there a song about **dreadful** Paul?" Laura asked her mother.

"Dreadful Paul?" Mama looked puzzled. "Where did you hear a song like that?"

"You know, Mama, we sing it at school. 'See, He breaks the prison wall. Throws aside the dreadful Paul . . .' That's what it says."

Mama looked questioningly at Big Sister Sharon.

"She means 'Mighty Army of the Young,' Mama!" Sharon explained. "Here's how it goes,

'Mighty army of the young,
Lift the voice in cheerful song.
Send the welcome word along,
Jesus lives.

'See, He breaks the prison wall,
Throws aside the dreadful pall,
Conquers death at once for all,
Jesus lives!'"

"Yes, I remember that song," said Mama, with a smile. "You see, Laura, it isn't talking about a person named Paul. The word in the song is spelled *p-a-l-l,* not *p-a-u-l* like the name *Paul.* It means 'gloom' or 'sadness.' Jesus takes our sadness away."

"But, Mama, there really is a dreadful Paul," Laura insisted. "He is in my room, but he's bigger than I am. He's a fourth-grade boy. And he pesters me all the time! Yesterday he put a dead animal's foot in my lunchbox, right beside my sandwich. And today he put in a possum's tail—a **nasty** old possum tail in my lunch, Mama! I thought it was a snake, and I screamed. And he just laughed."

"Where does he *get* stuff like that?" Sharon gasped.

"His big brother traps animals," Laura explained. "He can get all kinds of nasty things. He's mean. If he does anything like that tomorrow, I'm going to think of something to do to him that he doesn't like."

"No, you may not do anything mean to him," said Mama. "That would be wrong."

"But how can I make him stop?" asked Laura, almost in tears.

"Have you tried to be nice to him?"

"Not really," **admitted** Laura. "I haven't done anything. I try to stay away from him."

"If you try to get even with him, you will start something that will just make things worse and worse. I have a better idea," said Sharon. "Why don't you put something nice in his lunch box, Laura? Then maybe he will stop his mean tricks and be kind to you. What can she give Paul tomorrow, Mama?"

"That is a good idea. We have those candy bars Grandpa gave us," Mama said. "Laura, you may have an extra candy bar tomorrow to put into Paul's lunch box. That is the Christian way to treat those who are unkind to us."

"But I think I should at least tell the teacher," insisted Laura. "That dreadful Paul shouldn't get by with being so mean."

Mama shook her head. "The Bible teaches us that God's children should be kind to their enemies. Try the candy bar tomorrow and see what happens."

"All right," said Laura, at last. "I'll try it just this once."

The next day when the children opened their lunch boxes, Paul looked surprised. "Yippee! A candy bar! Who gave it to me? We don't have any candy bars at home." He looked around questioningly at the other children.

Laura's face turned pink. "I did," she admitted in a small voice. "I gave it to you."

Paul stared at her. His face turned bright red. "You

37

funny girl," he mumbled. "Well, thanks." He ripped the paper down and took a bite.

$$\sim \quad \sim \quad \sim \quad \sim \quad \sim$$

"What did Paul do at lunch today?" asked Mama as soon as Laura arrived home that afternoon.

Laura laughed. "He was so surprised and delighted to see the candy bar. They don't have any candy at home, so he knew someone gave it to him. Then he asked who did it, and I said I did.

"You should have seen how red he got, Mama! I thought maybe he would throw it back at me and say something nasty. But he didn't. He ate it first and said thank you too.

"The best part was that I didn't need to worry about his meanness. He stayed away from me the rest of the day."

$$\sim \quad \sim \quad \sim \quad \sim \quad \sim$$

"What has happened to 'the dreadful Paul'?" Sharon asked Laura at bedtime a few days later.

"Oh, it worked just like you said," Laura replied happily. "Paul never teases me any more. And today he helped me with my art project when the teacher said the fourth graders could help the third grade. He's not a dreadful Paul anymore. He's my friend."

– Mildred Martin

"O give thanks unto the LORD; for he is good."

– 1 Chronicles 16:34

The Last Pumpkin Seed

Spring and planting time had arrived. Ben and his father worked from sunup to sundown. Their small fields took a long time to finish because they planted the seeds by hand.

The wheat and all the garden seeds were in the ground. This **forenoon** Ben planted corn. His father went ahead, breaking up the hard earth with a heavy hoe.

As Ben worked, he did not think about corn. He thought about pumpkins.

This year there would not be any pumpkins. They had no seed.

"Oh, Father!" said Ben when they both stopped to rest for a while. "What do you suppose could have happened to the pumpkin seeds we saved last year?"

"Probably the mice got them," Father answered. "I am sorry we can't raise any pumpkins this year, but we must be thankful for the other seeds we have."

Ben agreed that they could live without pumpkins. But he did like pumpkin pies so much! He could not imagine Thanksgiving dinner without them.

That night, as the family sat by the blazing fire, Mother said, "Oh, Ben, please bring my button bag. Betsy's new **cloak** is ready for the buttons. I am sure I have three matching buttons the right size for this cloak. See if you can find them."

Ben took the bag from its nail near the fireplace. He emptied it out on the table and began sorting through them for three buttons just alike.

While pawing through the buttons, he found odd things that did not belong in the button bag. He saw a small ball of string, a few pins, a piece of leather, and a shiny marble he had lost long ago.

"What are these things doing in the button bag?" he asked.

"Oh," said Mrs. Chase with a chuckle, "I am always finding odd things that I think I should save, so I drop them into my apron pockets. I find more buttons than anything else. When I put them into the button bag, I don't notice that some other things go in too."

Just then Ben **spied** something else. "Look! Here is a pumpkin seed!" he cried.

"Really?" exclaimed Mother. "I must have dropped it into my pocket at one time or another. Thank the Lord that the mice didn't get into that button bag."

"Just one seed," Ben said. "But it might grow. I am going to plant it tomorrow. Maybe we'll have pumpkin pies after all."

The next forenoon Ben planted the seed. Day after day he watered it and prayed that it would grow. At last a tiny green leaf pushed through the earth.

"It's growing! It's growing!" Ben cried.

The family came running to see.

"Well," said Mr. Chase with a chuckle, "it looks fine now, but you better not count your pumpkins yet."

"I know," agreed Ben, "but I am going to ask the Lord for at least one. I will be much more thankful if we have pumpkin pies for Thanksgiving."

That week the plant grew several inches.

"See!" Ben said. "The Lord is making it grow into a big vine. We *will* have pumpkin pies. Just wait and see."

Ben carefully weeded and hoed his plant. Before long, three big yellow flowers bloomed among the large green pumpkin leaves. When the petals dried up, he saw three tiny green pumpkins.

All summer long the pumpkins grew until they were huge. Finally they turned yellow, then orange.

The day before Thanksgiving, Ben brought the biggest pumpkin to the house.

"This is for pies, Mother," he said. "I'll cut it up so that you can cook it. And you may be sure I'll save plenty of the seeds."

"That's too much pumpkin for one family," said Mother. "We don't need so many pies. With no one here for dinner but our family and Uncle Zeke, we can't eat more than two."

"I could eat a dozen pieces myself," said Ben. "Please make four or five. I'm sure someone will eat them. Anyway, four or five pies will show we are more thankful for that one pumpkin seed the Lord saved for us."

"All right, Ben," agreed Mother, "but I can't imagine what we will do with that many pies. We will be eating pumpkin pies every meal for a week."

"That's fine with me!" Ben laughed.

Ben cut up the pumpkin with a sharp knife. He added water to the kettle and put it over the fire. He stirred it often while it cooked. That afternoon his sister Betsy helped Mother make the pies.

On Thanksgiving Day, Mother showed the pies to Father.

"Look here," she said with a chuckle. "I can't imagine why I was so foolish as to bake all these pies yesterday for just ourselves. Ben talked me into it."

Just then someone knocked on the door. Father opened it and saw a tired-looking man.

"Come in, sir," he said to the stranger.

"Thank you," the man said. "I am Jim Frost. My family and I have traveled in our cart for many days. We plan to settle on a piece of land near here."

The stranger smiled at the friendly faces. Then he said, "At Gray's Crossing I heard that Zeke Chase often lets people stay with him. When I spied your house, I thought it might be Zeke's."

"No," said Mr. Chase, "but Zeke will soon be here. He is my brother. He's going to have Thanksgiving dinner with us. It would be a **pleasure** to have you and your family join our party."

"Thank you," said Mr. Frost. "I'll go out and tell my wife."

As they came into the house, Mrs. Frost and her daughter Sally smiled at the Chase family. "How kind of you to invite us to dinner. We are so tired of traveling," said Mrs. Frost.

Then she saw the pies all spread out.

"Oh," she said, "I see that you are expecting a lot of company. I'm sure you don't need any extra people."

"No, no," laughed Mother. "We aren't having any company except Zeke. My son wanted me to bake all these pumpkin pies to show God how thankful we were for that last pumpkin seed. He said someone would eat them, and he was right. How thankful I am now that I made so many and that you are here to help us eat them."

–*Eleanor Hammond*

"I was a stranger, and ye took me in."

– Matthew 25:35

A Strange Visitor

One day in the early fall, Mr. Chase had to go to Uncle Zeke's to help him with his farm work. Mother planned to go along to cook a good dinner for the men.

"I will take some ham, a loaf of bread, and some freshly **churned** butter," she said.

As they left, Father **shouldered** his gun.

"Perhaps we shall see a deer," he said. "Then we'll have something different to eat."

As soon as Mother and Father left, Ben and Betsy started their morning work. They put fresh candles in the candlesticks. They scrubbed the floor. They got vegetables ready for the next meal.

As Betsy stirred a pot of soup at the fireplace, she glanced out the back window. She caught her breath excitedly. "Ben! Ben!" she cried. "Look there!"

45

Ben ran to the window.

"Where?" he asked.

"There!" whispered Betsy, pointing toward the woods.

Out of the forest came a little boy. He looked about five years old. He had a round fat face, straight black hair, and shiny black eyes. He clutched a red blanket around his shoulders.

"It's an Indian boy," announced Ben. "We have never seen Indians near here before. I wonder where he came from."

"Let's ask him to come in," said Betsy. "He must be lost. Maybe he's hungry."

Ben and Betsy went to the back door and stepped out.

"Come in," Ben said to the Indian child.

For a moment the Indian just stood there. "Oh, Ben!" Betsy laughed. "He can't understand a word we say."

As they stood wondering what to do next, the little Indian walked toward them. He went right past them into the house.

When he saw the fireplace, his eyes shone. He walked up and held his hands close to the fire. He sniffed the air hungrily.

"I think he wants food," Ben said. "We must give him something to eat."

Ben got a piece of smoked ham from the **oaken** cupboard. Betsy took some vegetables from the

steaming pot that hung over the fire. Then she raked two roasted potatoes from the fireplace. She put all the food on a flat dish.

Ben and Betsy helped the little Indian take off his blanket.

All this time their visitor had not said one word. He sat down and looked at the steaming food on the dish. He picked up the ham in his hands and took a bite. Quickly he laid it down and reached out a hand to grab some hot vegetables.

"Wait!" cried Ben. "You'll burn yourself."

"I think we should help him," Betsy said. "He's not used to eating like we do."

So they took turns feeding their small visitor. First Ben put a bite of potato into his mouth. After the Indian had eaten that, Betsy gave him some other vegetables. Then they gave him a bite of ham and a bite of bread.

When the little boy had eaten everything on the dish, he smiled happily. He leaned against Ben's shoulder and closed his eyes.

"He's gone to sleep," Ben whispered.

Lifting their visitor carefully, Ben and Betsy managed to lay him on a narrow seat beside the **hearth**. They put a pillow under his head and covered him with his blanket.

Late in the afternoon, Betsy and Ben had finally washed all the dishes. They sat down and leaned against the narrow seat beside the hearth where the little boy slept. In a few minutes Ben and Betsy too, fell asleep.

Soon Mr. and Mrs. Chase came down the forest trail on their way home. When they were in sight of their house, they stopped and stared. Three Indians were looking in a back window of their cabin.

"Let's speak to them," said Mrs. Chase.

At the sound of her voice, an Indian with a headband of red and yellow feathers turned around. He made signs for the two white people to look in the window.

Mr. and Mrs. Chase came near and looked in the window. They saw the fire on the hearth. They saw Ben and Betsy sleeping near the fire and the Indian child asleep on the narrow seat.

The Indian with the feather headband said, "I am Chief White Bear." Then he continued to speak very slowly.

"My people come to this forest for two sleeps. My son leave tepee. We hunt him. We look in white man's house. My son sleeps here. White man's children take care of him. Chief White Bear much thankful."

Mr. and Mrs. Chase entered the house, followed by Chief White Bear and the two other Indians. Their footsteps woke the three children.

The chief's son jumped off the narrow seat and ran to his father, chattering in a strange language. At the chief's side he turned and looked at Ben and Betsy. His fat round face broke into a shy smile.

Ben and Betsy smiled back at him. "Come again," said Ben. The little Indian boy just looked at them. Then he took his father's hand and pulled him out the door. He was ready to go back to his own home.

—Dorothy Heiderstadt

Indian Children

Where we walk to school each day
Indian children used to play—
All about our native land,
Where the shops and houses stand.

And the trees were very tall,
And there were no streets at all,
Not a church and not a steeple—
Only woods and Indian people.

Only wigwams on the ground,
And at night bears prowling round—
What a different place today
Where we live and work and play!

—Annette Wynne

Look Out for the Blacksnakes

George sat reading his new storybook when his mother entered the room. "George, would you please run over to Mrs. Crosby's and ask her for my sleeve pattern?"

"Oh, Mother," said George, "it is so cold!"

"Nonsense! A big boy like you talking about the cold! Put on your cap and coat and go. I need that pattern soon."

"I am afraid of Jock," whined George.

"Jock is chained."

"He wasn't chained yesterday. I saw him running around the yard."

"Yes, but Mr. Crosby was with him then. He always is chained when no one is out with him. Run along and don't make any more excuses. You are getting to be a real **sluggard**."

"But, Mother, I'm lame. I fell yesterday and my leg really hurts."

"Lame! I saw you out playing football an hour ago. You can't be too lame to walk down the street. You have made three excuses, George. That's three too many! Now lay down your book and go at once." And Mother left the room.

George just sat there after his mother left until Grandpa looked sharply at him and said, "That's three snakes, George. Will you use them or kill them?"

George looked around with a very red face. When had Grandpa come in? "I'm going to kill them," he said, shutting his book with a bang. Without another word he left the room. Soon the top of his fur cap bobbed past the window.

"There he goes," said Grandpa to Mother, who had entered the room. "Have you noticed lately how George always runs when I speak of snakes? I told him a snake story the other day and it has done him good."

Here is the story Grandpa told:

Years ago, a boy called Tom had a bad habit. If someone asked him to do something he didn't want to do, he always made excuses. Most people would call him lazy.

His younger brother, Willie, was just the opposite.

Willie cheerfully obeyed and tried to see something pleasant in any job he had to do.

One summer when Tom was fourteen and Willie twelve, a family friend came to visit. Mr. Ames was a **wealthy** gentleman. In a few days he planned to sail for Europe on business. He also planned to spend some time sightseeing in some of the beautiful countries of Europe, but he did not want to go alone.

He spoke to Tom and Willie's parents about it. "I have two tickets and would like to take one of your boys with me. A boy can help me in many small ways as I travel. He would be good company when I go sightseeing. But I cannot decide which one it shall be. Tom is the older, but he has a lazy habit of making excuses when he doesn't want to do something."

"I know," agreed Father. "Perhaps this will be a good chance to teach him a lesson. Tomorrow I will give the boys a job. You watch what happens. Then take the boy who does it the way that suits you best."

The next day Father gave each boy a pail and asked them to go to the fields for huckleberries so Mother could make pies.

"Oh, good!" cried Willie. "Huckleberry pies! Let's go, Tom."

But Tom began as usual to make excuses. "I'm too tired. My head aches. It's too hot. There is a mean cow in that field we must cross. Anyway, it takes so long to pick enough huckleberries for pies."

"Go along now," said his father. "No more excuses."
So Tom went at last, **lagging** far behind Willie. He did
not know that Mr. Ames had heard all his excuses.

In about half an hour, Tom returned with the bottom
of his pail barely covered with berries.

"Are you done so soon? Where are
your berries?" asked Mother. "This
is not enough for pies."

Tom said, "I saw a big blacksnake
among the bushes and dared
not stay in the field another
minute. Anyway, I couldn't
find enough huckle-berries to
bother with." And Tom went out and
began to swing on the porch swing.

Willie came home much later with
his pail heaped with huckleberries.
Mr. Ames met him and asked, "What
all did you see in the field?"

"Nothing but beautiful
butterflies," replied Willie.

"No mean cows?"

"No mean cows," said Willie.

"No snakes? Tom said he
saw a blacksnake."

Willie laughed. "He told
me that too. I went right over

and looked among the bushes where he had been picking. I didn't see any snake or anything that looked like a snake. I told him that, but he kept on toward home. I stayed there and finished filling my pail. I found more huckleberries there than where I had been picking."

Willie wondered about the strange way his mother and father looked at Mr. Ames. In a short while he found out the reason.

And Tom found out too. He came upstairs to find Willie excitedly packing his suitcase to go to Europe with their friend. "Why didn't he pick me? I'm older than you," Tom asked in **keen** disappointment.

"I don't know," said Willie. "You'll have to ask him."

Tom did ask Mr. Ames.

Mr. Ames said, "I chose Willie because neither you nor I would have a pleasant time if you went. I watched the way you acted when your father sent you for huckleberries. I heard what you said when you came back. If I took you to Europe and wished you to do something a bit difficult, you would make excuses for not doing it. You would be too tired or too hot. Your head would ache. You would say it wasn't safe or would take too long. Likely you would see blacksnakes under every bush and want to come back and sit on the porch swing. I am sorry, Tom, but I don't think a sluggard would make a pleasant traveling **companion**.

"Willie will happily do everything I suggest. He will see nothing but butterflies and the other beautiful things that God has put on our earth. He will get right to work and work hard at anything I want him to do."

ॐ   ॐ   ॐ   ॐ   ॐ

Then Grandpa said, "I told this story to George to try to cure him of making excuses when he acted too lazy to do something.

"I said, 'Every time you obey without making an excuse, I'll call that *killing* a blacksnake, rather than *using* it as an excuse to **avoid** work.

"'But every time you invent an excuse for not doing as you are told, I'll call that looking for a blacksnake and using it to get out of work. Getting rid of that lazy habit will certainly please the Lord.'"

"Well, I hope it works," said Mother. "George truly has a bad habit of making excuses to get out of doing things he dislikes."

Just then George came in from Mr. Crosby's, red-cheeked and panting. He had been running.

"Here's your pattern, Mother," he said with a smile.

"Well," said Grandpa, "it's pretty cold out there. Did your ears freeze, George?"

George laughed and said, "No, sir."

"You didn't get very badly bitten by the dangerous dog, did you?"

"No, sir."

"Have you gotten over your lameness? I hope you didn't make that poor leg worse by running like that."

George laughed again and said, "The leg is all right now, Grandpa. It is so cold out there that I think we likely can go skating tonight."

"Oh, now you are seeing the butterflies," said Grandpa. "Aren't you glad you killed those three snakes?"

"Yes, sir," replied George. "I plan to be on the lookout for blacksnakes. It really is more fun to kill snakes than to use them as excuses."

–adapted

> *"And whatsoever ye do, do it heartily, as to the Lord, and not unto men."*
>
> – Colossians 3:23

Whatever You Do

"There, that is good enough," said Herb, throwing down the shoe brush. "My shoes don't look very good, but who cares? It doesn't matter. No one looks at them anyway."

"Whatever your hand finds to do, do it as well as you can. Then God will bless you," said a serious but pleasant voice behind him.

Herb started and turned to face his father. His face turned a guilty red, and he moved the shoes so his father could not see them. But his father picked them up and **inspected** them on all sides.

"Herb, these shoes do not look good to me. Take your brush and do them again. This time make them shine. When you have done the job right, come to me in the library."

"Yes, sir," replied Herb. He grabbed the brush and started working again. He felt very much ashamed that Pa had heard what he said and had seen the careless job he had done.

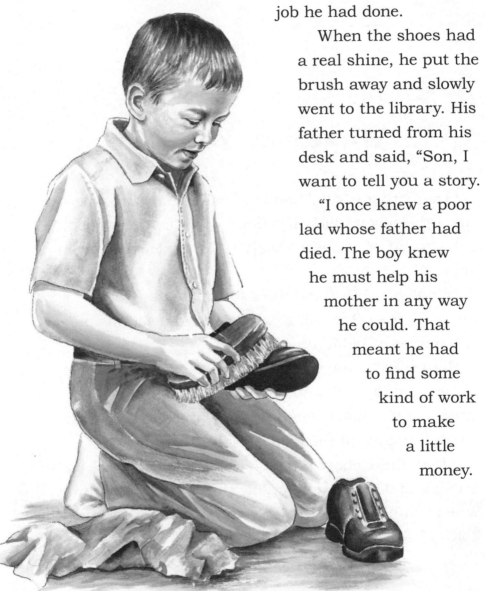

When the shoes had a real shine, he put the brush away and slowly went to the library. His father turned from his desk and said, "Son, I want to tell you a story.

"I once knew a poor lad whose father had died. The boy knew he must help his mother in any way he could. That meant he had to find some kind of work to make a little money.

"His mother had told him one thing over and over from the time he was a little chap. 'Whatever your hand finds to do, do it as well as you can. Then God will bless you.' She had seen to it that he did his little jobs around the house as well as a child could do them.

"Well, this young boy finally found a job helping in the kitchen of a very wealthy man. There he tried hard to do everything well, no matter how **unimportant** it seemed.

"When the cook told him to take the garbage to the pigs, he made sure to throw it well into the pen. He wanted no peelings or anything else to get hung on the fence. Then he **rinsed** out the pan at the yard pump before taking it back to the kitchen.

"When the housekeeper told him to sweep the porch, he swept the steps and the walk as well.

"When he brought in coal, he filled the bucket as full as possible. He cleaned up any he spilled. Even when he scrubbed kettles that would only get black again, he made them shine.

"And God did bless him. His **employer** noticed the way he always did things as well as possible. He soon took him out of the kitchen and made him an office boy in his store.

"There he worked the same way. He emptied the trash cans every morning whether they were full or not. He swept just as carefully under the counters where no one could see as he did the main floor. When sent on an **errand**, he took care to do it right. He went and came without wasting time.

"He was not a perfect boy. He made many mistakes as he learned each new job. Some things he never could do very well; but he stuck with his mother's rule: 'Whatever your hand finds to do, do it as well as you can. Then God will bless you.'

"Often it seemed silly to do a perfect job on something that really didn't matter. Many times his employer never inspected his work anyway. But he remembered Mother had told him that the job was not the important thing. The important thing was to make a habit of doing everything as well as he could.

"Finally his employer made the young man head clerk in the store. Several years later he asked him to become a partner in the business. Now that man, under God's blessing, has all the money he needs. And he is eager that his son Herb learns to live by the same rule his father followed."

"Why, Pa, were you that boy? Were you and Grandmother really poor when you were little?" exclaimed Herb.

"Yes, my son, so poor that in order to keep from going hungry, I had to go away from home and learn to black other people's boots and carry out their garbage and other jobs like that.

"By doing these little tasks well, as the Bible teaches, I was soon given more important jobs.

"But even when I was poor, I was always happy at work. I was not afraid when my employer came around while I was working. I didn't feel guilty when he inspected the job I had done. I was satisfied that I had done my best. That was part of the blessing."

Herb understood that very well, for he remembered how guilty he had felt when Pa had discovered him at work only half an hour ago. *If I had been putting a real shine on those shoes,* he thought, *I would not have been ashamed for Pa to see them.*

"One more thing, Herb," his father said. "Your grandmother found that good rule for work in a book. The wisest man who ever lived wrote that rule."

"You mean Solomon," said Herb.

"Yes. You will find the rule in Ecclesiastes 9:10. It would be a good verse to memorize."

"Well, since you told me that story about yourself, Pa, I am sure I'll always remember what the verse means," said Herb. "And after this, I'm going to try to work just like you did when you were my age."

–adapted

"Be of good cheer: it is I; be not afraid."

– Mark 6:50

Is It a Ghost?

45. And straightway he constrained his disciples to get into the ship, and to go to the other side before unto Bethsaida, while he sent away the people.

46. And when he had sent them away, he **departed** into a mountain to pray.

47. And when even was come, the ship was in the midst of the sea, and he alone on the land.

48. And he saw them **toiling** in rowing; for the wind was **contrary** unto them: and about the fourth watch of the night he cometh unto them, walking upon the sea, and would have passed by them.

49. But when they saw him walking upon the sea, they supposed it had been a spirit, and cried out:

50. For they all saw him, and were troubled. And immediately he talked with them, and saith unto them, Be of good cheer: it is I; be not afraid.

51. And he went up unto them into the ship; and the wind **ceased**: and they were sore amazed in themselves beyond measure, and wondered.

– Mark 6:45-51

I Wish I Were a Rich Grown-Up

"I wish I were a man," said Johnny Marks to himself one winter morning as he lay in bed. "I wish I were grown-up so I could do a lot of good for other people."

Johnny lived a long time ago before there were cars. In those days if you were rich, you rode in a **carriage** drawn by horses. If you were poor, you walked.

At the breakfast table Johnny said the same thing. "If only I were a man I could work and be rich. Then I would buy food and clothes and toys for poor boys and girls. And I would see to it that they had wood and coal to keep their houses warm. Think of all the good I could do if I were a rich grown-up! I could ride around in a carriage and find poor people to help."

"You can help poor children even if you aren't rich. Surely you know some poor children at your school," said Father.

"And you can do a lot of good without being grown-up," said his mother. "There are many things that only a boy can do—things you would never have a chance to do if you were grown. And remember that rich people who ride in carriages need help sometimes too. Money can't do everything."

"If you want to do good when you grow up, you should start to practice now. Being helpful is mostly a matter of habit," said Father.

"I can't think of a single thing a poor boy like me could do," said Johnny.

"Keep your eyes open," said his father.

"Keep your ears open," said his mother.

On the way to school, Johnny thought about what his parents had said.

He decided it would be fun to practice being a rich grown-up. It would be fun to see what he could do, even though he had no money and was still just a boy.

"Ears and eyes open," he told himself as he walked along in the snow. But he neither saw nor heard anything until he turned in at the school. There he saw two big boys come laughing around the corner and run into the building.

Then he heard an angry, tearful voice shouting, "You

mean, mean boys. I am going to tell your teacher on you!"

Johnny went around the side of the building. There he saw a small girl in a ragged sweater and no cap getting up from the snow. Around her were scattered books and papers.

"They knocked them out of my hands and pushed me down," she sobbed. It was Polly Pringle. Her voice **quavered** with the cold. During the winter she never wore more than a sweater to school and, sometimes, no stockings. She was shivering now.

Johnny quickly gathered the scattered papers from the snow and **shuffled** them together neatly. "And here are your other books and your lunch box. I'll carry them in for you if you want me to, Polly."

"All right," said the little girl, sniffing and wiping her eyes on her sleeve. "Those mean boys won't dare to pick on me again if you go with me."

Johnny walked with Polly to the door of her room. There he handed her the rest of her things. She was still half crying and did not say anything as she took them.

But Johnny didn't care. As he went on to his own room he thought, *There really are poor children in our school. I never noticed them before, but I will now. I can practice on them every day.*

On the way home that evening, Johnny passed the fine house of Mrs. Vander Van. He heard a thin voice

calling, "Pepper, Pepper. Come, Pepper dear."

There on the wide porch stood a little old lady leaning on a cane. She was wrapped in a thick white **shawl**. "Pepper, Pepper, where are you? You will catch a cold out here."

Then Johnny saw a black poodle dog outside the **hedge**. It wore a huge red bow around its neck. The little dog had tried to get back into the yard through a hole in the hedge, but the bow had caught. Now the little fellow could not go in or out.

In no time Johnny had freed the small shivering creature and put him under his warm coat. Then he opened the gate and went up to the porch.

"Here is your dog, Ma'am," he said. "He was caught in the hedge and could not get free."

"Oh, Pepper dear," quavered the little old lady, taking the poodle and tucking him under her shawl. "Why did you run away? I could never have gone out to look for you. You would have frozen to death in no time.

"Now, my good lad, step into the house and I will pay you for saving my darling Pepper." Mrs. Vander Van **hobbled** to the wide front door and opened it.

"No, thank you, Ma'am. I do not want to be paid for helping you. I am glad I happened by just now. I hope your little dog will be all right."

Johnny went down the steps and headed for home. Soon he began to whistle. "Mother and Father were right," he said to himself. "If I had been a grown-up I could not have helped poor Polly Pringle, because I would not have been in the school yard and heard her crying.

"And if I had been a rich man, I could not have helped Mrs. Vander Van. I would have been riding by in a carriage instead of walking. I would not have seen her little dog caught in the hedge.

"So I can indeed do good to the poor and the rich even though I am only a boy with no money. I don't need to be a rich grown-up if I keep my ears and eyes open."

—adapted

In this poem, a little girl is dreaming about having her own house. Do you think she will be a good housekeeper when she grows up?

The Shiny Little House

I wish, how I wish, that I had a little house,
With a mat for the cat and a hole for the
    mouse,
And a clock going "tock" in a corner of the
    room,
And a kettle, and a cupboard, and a big birch
    broom.

To school in the morning the children off
    would run,
And I'd give them a kiss and a penny and a
    bun.
But directly they had gone from this little
    house of mine,
I'd clap my hands and snatch a cloth and
    shine, shine, shine.

I'd shine all the knives, all the windows and
    the floors,
All the grates, all the plates, all the handles
    on the doors,
Every fork, every spoon, every lid, and every
    tin,
Till everything was shining like a new bright
    pin.

At night, by the fire, when the children were
    in bed,
I'd sit and I'd knit, with a cap upon my head,
And the kettles and the saucepans, they
    would shine, shine, shine,
In this tweeny little, cozy little house of mine!

– Nancy M. Hayes

Do-As-You-Please Land

"Mama," asked Harry, as he came in from school, "may I go coasting?"

"Yes, Harry, as soon as you have cleared the snow off the paths around the house."

"Oh, dear!" said Harry impatiently, as he looked out the window. "I always have to be digging snow or doing some other work. I wish we wouldn't have this old snow. No, I don't wish that. I wish it would fall only on the coasting hill. No, that wouldn't do either, because then we couldn't have snowballing at school.

"But I do think boys have it hard. They always have to be doing things for other people."

"Do you think boys do more for other people than others do for them?" asked Mama.

"Yes, indeed, Mama. We have paths to clear and wood to carry and ashes to take out and the mail to get from the box and so many other errands to run—always things that boys must do. Girls have it easy. I wish there were a Do-As-You-Please Land. I would move there right now!"

"If you mean a land where each one pleased only himself, I think such a place should be called Selfish Land. How would you like it if no one did anything for you? How would you like to do everything for yourself?"

"I'd like it fine if I didn't have to do anything for others."

"Well, then," said Mama, "you may pretend you are in Do-As-You-Please Land from now on. But remember, don't expect anyone to do anything for you. We will go to Do-As-You-Please Land, too."

"Hurrah!" shouted Harry, jumping up in delight. "No more errands forever! No one has to help me go coasting. I can do that myself."

"Change your **trousers** before you go," reminded Mama. "Oh, sorry," she said with a laugh. "I forgot. You have gone to Do-As-You-Please Land. You may do as you please about changing your trousers."

Harry laughed too. But he was so pleased to be free from rules that he did change his trousers. However, he did not hang them up as he was supposed to do. He just gave them a **fling** into a corner of his bedroom.

Away he ran for his cap, coat, mittens, and boots. Soon he joined the boys on the hill. He coasted until dark and then **trudged** home, tired and hungry.

He dropped his wet coat, mittens, cap, and boots on the back porch. Then he rushed into the warm kitchen. But he stopped at the dining room door and stared. Nothing was on the table. Mama stood at the sink washing dishes.

"Oh, Mama, why didn't you call me for supper?" he asked.

"Well," said Mama, going on with the dishes, "I decided to visit Do-As-You-Please Land too. I just didn't feel like making anything for you tonight, so there wasn't any use calling you. The rest of us ate a while ago."

Without saying a word, Harry began looking for something to eat. He helped himself to what he could find. But it was a cold and lonely supper, with the rest of the family laughing and talking around the cozy living room fire.

꒱ ꒱ ꒱ ꒱ ꒱

"Where is my place?" Harry asked the next morning as he came into the kitchen for breakfast. Then he remembered that no one had to do anything for him. He brought a plate and spoon for himself and sat down. But no one passed anything to him. He had to reach for what he wanted or get up and walk around the table for it. Long before he was finished eating, tears stood in his eyes because no one seemed to care whether he had anything to eat or not. But he said nothing.

Getting ready for school was worse. Harry had noticed that his lunch box was not with the others, packed, and ready to go. It sat on the counter where he had put it the evening before. He opened it to face the balled-up wax paper, half-eaten sandwich, and black banana peelings from yesterday's lunch. Without a word he dumped everything into the trash can.

He didn't know where Mama kept the lunch things and he couldn't ask her. He knew she had gone to Do-As-You-Please Land and thought maybe she didn't like to make lunches any more than he did. So he put a few things into his box as fast as he could.

When he went to get dressed for school, he found his school trousers, which had lain in the corner all night, too damp and wrinkled to wear. He had to put on another pair.

When he came downstairs, his coat and cap and mittens and boots were not hanging warm and dry behind the stove where Mama usually put them. Without thinking, he asked, "Mama, didn't you hang up my school coat and things?"

"No, dear," answered Mama, pleasantly. "Did you forget I am living in Do-As-You-Please Land? I don't enjoy taking care of other people's wet things. Your clothes are where you left them, I guess."

Harry rushed to the back porch. His coat, cap, and gloves were frozen stiff. He put them on because they were the only ones he had.

He couldn't find his book and was afraid to ask his mother to help him hunt for it. Shivering and upset, he hurried to school all alone. Mama had not made the other children wait for him as she usually did.

All through that long day the words of his mother kept running through Harry's mind: "If you have gone to Do-As-You-Please Land, don't expect anyone to do anything for you."

He thought of all that had happened and began to wonder if, after all, boys really did more for their mothers than their mothers did for them.

He kept thinking about it as he trudged home from school—alone again. At last he said to himself, "I guess I am a pretty selfish, lazy boy. I'm afraid Mama thinks so too. But I know what I'll do the minute I get home. Mama will soon find out that I can be different than that when I make up my mind."

As soon as he reached home, he ran to his mother and said, "Mama, do you want a boy to dig snow and bring in wood and run errands without fussing? I have just gotten back from Do-As-You-Please Land. I want to try to please other people now."

"Back already!" cried Mama. "What made you change your mind and come back so soon?"

"Well," said Harry, "it might have been fun if you had not decided to move there too. But I found out that you do more for me than I could ever do for you. So if you need a boy, I'm the boy for you, Mama."

"I do need a boy. I like my own Harry better than any other. I have left Do-As-You-Please Land too, for it is a lonely, selfish place, isn't it?"

"Yes, it is," said Harry, thinking of his lonely, unhappy day. "So just give me a job, Mama, and I'll show you I mean to stay as far away from that place as I can."

–adapted

A Hero for Nero

Howard Briggs admired bravery more than anything else. He would rather be brave than strong or smart or rich. And he thought he *was* brave for a nine-year-old.

"Don't you think I am pretty brave, Mother?" he asked one day. "I'm not afraid of the dark. I'm not afraid of stray dogs. I'm not afraid to take bad-tasting medicine. And I'm not even afraid to do new things."

"No, dear," said his mother with a smile. "If you are not afraid of those things, it does not take bravery to do them. Bravery is doing what you *ought* to do even when you are afraid. That's what makes a true hero."

Howard did not think his mother was right about that, because all his friends thought he was the bravest boy in school.

However, Howard was a real **coward** about one thing. He feared being punished. If he did anything wrong, would he tell his parents or teacher what had happened? No, he would not. Instead, he said nothing at all. He hoped no one would ever find out what he had done.

Of course, Howard spent many miserable hours until his **misdeeds** were discovered. Often, too, he would be punished harder because he had not reported what had happened. How could such a brave boy be such a coward?

Now you might think that since he was so afraid of being punished, he would never disobey his parents. But that was not always the case.

One day when his mother was gone, Howard went into the living room bouncing his ball. Mother had told him not to bounce his ball there, but he couldn't see why not. What did it matter? What could happen?

Very shortly, Howard found out what could happen. He bounced his ball and missed catching it. The ball hit the arm of a chair and bounced sideways onto the table.

CRASH! There in many pieces lay his mother's beautiful blue china vase. It was her favorite vase, given to her by her grandmother long ago.

Howard was terribly frightened. He grabbed his ball and ran out of the living room and out of the house.

Later on, his dog Nero was in the house and discovered the open living room door. Nero was not supposed to be in that room, but he loved to sleep on the soft sofa. When he saw the open door, in he padded and up on the sofa he jumped. Soon he was sound asleep.

Howard stayed outside until Mother returned. He knew he should tell her immediately what he had done. But he was too big a coward. He followed her into the house. Then he went upstairs, hoping she would not go into the living room for a long, long time.

However, Mother soon noticed the open door. Going in, she immediately saw the broken vase and Nero on the sofa.

"Nero, you bad, bad dog," she cried. "You know you are not supposed to be in here! Now you have broken my precious, precious vase! You simply *must* learn to stay out of here."

Howard, coming down the stairs, saw his mother preparing to go outside.

"What are you going to do, Mother?"

"I am going to lock Nero in the shed the rest of the day. He got into the living room and broke my beautiful blue vase." Mother marched in and took Nero by the collar.

Howard could not **bear** to think of Nero being punished for something he had not done. "Don't, Mother," he cried. "Don't punish Nero. He didn't break your vase. I did."

Mother was much astonished, and of course she had to hear the whole story. And she had to punish Howard for his disobedience.

Afterward she said, "Howard, you were a hero to confess what you had done, instead of letting Nero be punished. He could never have told on you."

"I thought of that, Mother," said Howard quietly. "But I couldn't bear to see Nero punished for what I had done."

Howard never forgot how hard it had been to tell Mother the truth to save Nero. Now he knew his mother had spoken the truth when she said, "Bravery is doing what you ought to do, even when you are afraid."

–adapted

> *"Thou shalt heap coals of fire on his head."*
>
> – Romans 12:20

Coals of Fire

One bright day six merry friends headed out of the village for the woods.

"Hurrah for a sunny Saturday!" cried Neil.

"Hurrah for autumn!" cried Ned.

"Hurrah for hickory nuts!" cried Roy.

"Hurrah for a nutting party!" cried the others.

A mile out of town they saw ahead of them a boy slowly pushing a cart up the hill.

"There's Billy with his old cart," said Roy.

Billy was the son of a poor **widow**. Day after day he plodded about with his cart, running errands for people and doing things to earn a little money. Since his father had died, Billy worked hard to take care of his mother as well as he could.

Sometimes the cart held vegetables he had raised to sell. Sometimes it held trash he had been hired to take to the town dump. Other times he delivered bundles for someone in the village. Billy stayed busy hauling some kind of load in his little cart. He had no time for the fun of hunting hickory nuts.

"I wonder what he has in it this time," said Roy.

"Let's play a trick on him," suggested Ned. "Let's catch up with him and tip the cart over."

"Yes, let's. It's probably full of trash and will make a beautiful mess."

The six boys trotted along the dusty road as quietly as they could, but Billy heard them coming. He saw they intended **mischief** and held fast to the handle of the cart.

"Apples!" shouted Roy when they saw what Billy had. "Won't they roll just dandy!"

"Over with the cart!" cried Ned.

"Please, boys, leave me alone," cried Billy. "Shame on you! Six against one!"

But the boys only laughed as they surrounded him. Roy and Ned **seized** his arms. One seized the cart handle. The three others took hold of the cart, crowding together on one side to upset it. Over it went, and out rolled the apples as the boys gave the cart a big shove down the hill.

"Ouch! Oh, ouch! My foot!" cried Neil, sinking to the ground.

In the struggle to dump the apples, his foot had

caught in the **spokes** of the wheel and was badly twisted as the cart was shoved downhill.

"What's wrong?"

"What happened?"

"Let's see it."

"Can you walk?"

Neil tried to get up, but sank back groaning when he put his foot on the ground. "I can't."

Two boys put their shoulders under his arms and helped Neil to hop to the grass beside the road. There he sank down again, gritting his teeth to keep from groaning out loud.

His friends stood around him helplessly.

"What shall we do now?" asked Roy.

"Perhaps it will feel better if I rest a while," said Neil. "You fellows go on. I'll come after a while."

"Shouldn't we try to get you home?" asked one.

"No, that would take too long," said Neil. "You just go on. I'll be all right."

"We hate to leave you here like this," said Ned. "But it's the only day we'll have for getting nuts. The squirrels will have them all by next Saturday."

Neil really didn't think they intended to go off and leave him, but they did. Waving good-bye, they entered the woods further up the hill.

By now Neil's foot was swelling fast and was hurting worse all the time. He could not help groaning in pain and disappointment as he watched his friends disappear.

In the excitement, no one had paid the least bit of attention to Billy. Partway down the hill the widow's son had righted the cart. Neil saw him gathering the scattered apples, wiping off the dust on his patched trousers.

When Billy looked up and saw Neil sitting alone beside the road, he came up to him.

"Are you much hurt?" he asked.

"I'm afraid so," replied Neil with **downcast** eyes. "It's my foot. Never mind. I'll just wait till the boys come back. They'll help me home or get someone to fetch me."

Neil could not look at Billy. He was embarassed and sorry now that he had helped upset the cart that had caused the **injury** to his foot. His friends had gone off to have fun, leaving him alone to face the boy they had treated so meanly.

Billy stood there a moment, then, saying no more, went for his cart. He took out the apples and piled them beside the road. Then he backed the cart as close as possible to where the injured boy lay.

"Now, up with you," he said, putting a strong arm under Neil's and helping him into the cart.

"It isn't a very fine carriage," he said as he seized the handle and started for the village. "But it's better than walking, I guess. It looks to me like that foot of yours needs attention right away. I'll try to miss the bumps as much as possible."

～   ～   ～   ～   ～

"Mother," said Neil that night as he lay with his foot all bandaged and propped up. "I know now what you mean about heaping coals of fire on a person's head. Are they ever burning me! I would rather have had Billy hit me with all his apples than be so kind after the way we treated him. That wouldn't have hurt half as much."

"Billy obeyed what the Bible teaches about returning good for evil," said his mother. "I'm sorry you and your friends didn't. You hurt Billy. You hurt me. And you hurt yourself the worst of all—doing something you thought would be fun. I can't believe you all were so mean to a poor widow's son."

"But, Mother, we weren't trying to be mean. We just thought how funny those apples would look rolling down the road.

"I did think about Billy at first. I almost said, 'No, we'd better not,' when Ned suggested it. But I was too much of a coward to try to stop them. It probably wouldn't have done any good anyhow. It's awfully hard, Mother, not to go along with things your friends do."

"I know, son, but sometimes you must be different if you want to do right. Even though you couldn't stop the other boys, you didn't need to help them dump the cart. If you had been brave enough for that, you wouldn't be lying here now with that hurt foot."

"I thought of that. And Billy knows I am sorry, because I told him so on the way home. But I still feel terrible about the whole thing.

"Believe me, Mother, I'm going to be kind to Billy after this, no matter what the other boys do. Somehow playing mean tricks on someone doesn't sound like fun anymore."

–adapted

> *"O Lᴏʀᴅ my God, I will give thanks*
> *unto thee for ever."*
> – Psalm 30:12

The Most Important Thing

On Monday morning Mrs. Beck suggested, "Since this is the week before Thanksgiving Day, let's spend a little time telling about things we've learned about early Thanksgiving Days. Who'll start us off?"

Many hands waved in the air. The teacher called on Peter. "The Pilgrims had a Thanksgiving Day feast in America to celebrate the harvest," Peter said, "and invited the Indians."

Marilyn was next. "One of the main things the Pilgrims served at this feast was succotash, an Indian dish made of corn and beans cooked together."

Beth claimed that wild geese, wild ducks, clams, eels, and ocean fish, as well as wild turkeys, had been on that first Thanksgiving Day **menu**.

When Jerry's turn came, he asked the class a question: "What is the most important thing to have at a

Thanksgiving Day dinner?"

Everyone shouted, "Turkey!"

Jerry smiled. "No, that's not it."

Mrs. Beck held up her hand for silence. "We don't have any more time to discuss Thanksgiving today," she said. "But think about Jerry's question, and we'll try to guess the answer tomorrow."

During recess some of the children tried to get Jerry to tell them the answer. Others shouted out what they thought the answer was. But Jerry just kept shaking his head and smiling. He was glad when the bell rang again.

On Tuesday morning Mrs. Beck selected Jane to answer Jerry's question. Even before she stood up, Jane cried, "Pumpkin pie! Thanksgiving wouldn't be Thanksgiving without pumpkin pie."

"No, it's not pumpkin pie."

"Mincemeat pie!" someone guessed.

Jerry repeated, "No."

Then Steven had a turn. "I know it's cranberry sauce. It has to be cranberry sauce," he insisted.

"But it isn't cranberry sauce," Jerry quickly replied.

Guesses of mashed potatoes, sweet potatoes, and gravy also proved to be wrong.

Looking puzzled herself, Mrs. Beck told the children they would have to try again on Wednesday morning. "Think hard now," she **urged**. "Tomorrow will be our last chance to answer Jerry's question correctly, because the next day is Thanksgiving Day." She smiled at Jerry. "I think we need a hint, Jerry."

Jerry stroked his chin, thinking hard. "All right," he said. "This is the hint: My daddy says no Thanksgiving dinner is really complete without it."

ॐ   ॐ   ॐ   ॐ   ॐ

Wednesday morning found the classroom a noisy place. Everyone wanted to answer Jerry's question. Mrs. Beck picked Sally first. "I'm positive my answer is right," Sally announced. "It's stuffing—you know, that lumpy bread stuff that's baked inside the turkey."

Everyone groaned when Jerry said, "The answer is not stuffing."

"Rolls and butter!" Fred suggested.

Jerry shook his head.

"Baked ham!" cried a voice from the back of the room. "Or roast duck or chicken."

"Salad!"

"Fruit cake!"

"Peas and carrots!"

"Roasted chestnuts!"

"Fruit!"

"Coffee! Tea! Milk!"

The children were guessing wildly now, but Jerry just

kept repeating, "No. No. No."

Finally, raising her hand for silence, Mrs. Beck said, "Jerry, how about one last hint?"

This time Jerry had his hint all ready. "Some people say that it has to be part of the Thanksgiving dinner or else the food wouldn't taste good."

There was much whispering and mumbling and bobbing of heads. Suddenly Donna clapped her hands. "I've got it!" she squealed. "It's salt! Hardly anything tastes good without salt."

"Salt is not the answer," Jerry said.

"We give up!" a girl's voice called out. Everyone agreed. They had run out of answers.

Mrs. Beck put her hand on Jerry's shoulder. "Well, Jerry, it looks like you've **stumped** us. What is the most important thing to have at a Thanksgiving Day dinner?"

"A prayer of thanks," Jerry answered.

"No fair," someone said.

"It's true. Daddy says no Thanksgiving dinner is complete without it, because giving thanks is the reason for it all. And," Jerry quickly added, "some people really do believe that Thanksgiving dinner wouldn't taste good without the prayer. My parents do. And so do I." Jerry sat down.

After a moment's silence, Mrs. Beck said, "Jerry is right. Being thankful and thanking God is the most important part of any Thanksgiving dinner. It is too bad that for three days all we could think about was food. It is too bad that none of us thought about the One who gives us all those good things. Thank you, Jerry, for reminding us.

"Let me remind you, too, that feasting was not the reason for the first Thanksgiving. The Pilgrims planned the day as a time to thank God for giving them a good harvest.

"Now, class," continued Mrs. Beck, "on Thanksgiving Day tomorrow, how many of you will remember to include the most important thing?"

Jerry smiled from ear to ear as hands went up all over the classroom.

—*Rosalyn Hart Finch*

Do you go to your grandparents' home on Thanksgiving Day? If you do, you probably don't travel the way the family in this poem traveled.

Thanksgiving Day

Over the river and through the wood,
   To Grandfather's house we go;
      The horse knows the way
To carry the sleigh
   Through the white and drifted snow.

Over the river and through the wood—
   Oh, how the wind does blow!
      It stings the toes
And bites the nose,
   As over the ground we go.

Over the river and through the wood,
   To have a first-rate play,
      Hear the bells ring,
"Ting-a-ling-ding!"
   Hurrah for Thanksgiving Day!

Over the river and through the wood—
   Trot fast, my dapple-gray!
      Spring over the ground,
Like a hunting hound!
   For this is Thanksgiving Day.

Over the river and through the wood,
   And straight through the barnyard gate.
      We seem to go
Extremely slow—
   It is so hard to wait!

Over the river and through the wood—
   Now Grandmother's cap I spy!
      Hurrah for the fun!
Is the pudding done?
   Hurrah for the pumpkin pie!

                        –*Lydia Maria Child*

> *"Come hither, and hear the words*
> *of the LORD your God."*
>
> – Joshua 3:9

Who Needs a Bridge?

9. And Joshua said unto the children of Israel, Come hither, and hear the words of the LORD your God.

11. Behold, the ark of the covenant of the Lord of all the earth passeth over before you into Jordan.

12. Now therefore take you twelve men out of the tribes of Israel, out of every tribe a man.

13. And it shall come to pass, as soon as the **soles** of the feet of the priests that **bear** the ark of the LORD, the Lord of all the earth, shall rest in the waters of Jordan, that the waters of Jordan shall be cut off from the waters that come down from above; and they shall stand upon an heap.

14. And it came to pass, when the people removed from their tents, to pass over Jordan, and the priests bearing the ark of the covenant before the people;

15. And as they that bare the ark were come unto Jordan, and the feet of the priests that bare the ark were dipped in the brim of the water, (for Jordan overfloweth all his banks all the time of harvest,)

16. That the waters which came down from above stood and rose up upon an heap very far from the city Adam, that is beside Zaretan: and those that came down toward the sea of the plain, even the salt sea, failed, and were cut off: and the people passed over right against Jericho.

17. And the priests that bare the ark of the covenant of the LORD stood firm on dry ground in the midst of Jordan, and all the Israelites passed over on dry ground, until all the people were passed clean over Jordan.

–Joshua 3:9, 11-17

The World's Biggest Pet

Thailand is a country far across the ocean, not far from China. It is a country of mountains and rivers; of rice fields and tin mines; of jungles and teak forests; of elephants, wild pigs, crocodiles, snakes, and birds.

Thailand has some big cities where many people live. But most of Thailand's people live in small villages. Because Thailand gets much rain, the people in some places build their houses high above the ground on **stilts** made of wood from the teak tree. The stilts keep the houses high and dry so they do not get full of water, and the oily teakwood does not rot when the floods come.

One morning years ago, in a little mountain village near the teak forest, a boy lay sleeping. His father bent over him. "Come, Son-sak."

Son-sak sat up. "What is it, Pol?" (*Pol* is the Thai word for *father*.)

"I need you to come help us work in the forest today," Father answered.

If you could have listened to Father and Son-sak talking as they set off with other men from the village, you very likely would not have been able to understand them. They spoke the Thai language. It is quite different from English.

In the Thai language, each word can have as many as five different meanings. The tone of voice in which a word is said gives it its different meanings. Saying a word in a high tone of voice makes it mean one thing, and saying it in a lower tone of voice makes it mean something else.

Here is an example of how tone of
voice changes the meaning of a word in
the language of Thailand.

naa spoken in a high tone means *aunt, uncle,*
or your mother's younger *brother* or *sister.*

naa spoken in a falling tone means *face,* or *in
front of,* or *next,* or *season* (weather).

naa spoken in a rising tone means *thick.*

naa spoken in a middle tone means *rice patties.*

"Will we be working near the river today, Pol?" asked Son-sak.

"No," said Father. "We just ringed those trees last week. Now we will start working farther back in the forest, away from the river. We cut a ring of bark off the trees farther back several years ago, and they are ready to cut now."

Workers in the teak forests do not just go into the forest and begin cutting trees. Before they cut down a tree, they cut off a wide ring of the bark all the way around the tree. Without the bark, the tree cannot get the water and food it needs to live. In several years, it dies. Then it is easier for the men to cut the trees and float them down the river.

When they reached the forest, several of the men began chopping down the dead trees. Son-sak cut the branches off the trunks and helped cut the trees into shorter logs. The forest was soon filled with the sweet smell of teakwood.

All day the men worked in the forest. When they left that evening, there were many logs stacked neatly among the trees. "Tomorrow we will bring the elephants," said Father. "They can drag the logs to the river."

So the next morning Son-sak set off for the forest riding high on the back of his pet elephant Phet. When they reached the place where the logs were stacked, Father rode over to Son-sak.

"Start with this stack of logs," he said. "Phet knows what to do, but if he gets lazy, **prod** him with your stick."

Son-sak fastened a log to Phet's harness with a long, heavy chain. Phet had worked in the teak forest before, so he knew what to do next. He clump-clump-clumped his way down to the river, dragging the log behind him. Then back he went for another log.

Before long there was a slowly growing pile of logs beside the river where Phet's trunk and tusks had stacked them. Back and forth, back and forth they went. Son-sak talked to Phet as they clumped along. "Did you know that Thailand has more teak forests than any other country in the world?"

Phet said nothing.

"Well, it does," said Son-sak. "And do you know that I like you better than any other elephant in the world?"

Still Phet said nothing.

"Well, I do," said Son-sak. "And do you know how important you are? How could we do this job without your help? We could never carry all these logs to the river. Then how could we float them down the river to the sawmill?"

Phet did not answer, but someone else did. Father had heard Son-sak speaking. "Yes, we are glad for the elephants, but it is time to give them a rest now. Even strong elephants shouldn't work all day without a break."

So Phet and Son-sak stopped working. While they rested, Phet ate his lunch of banana leaves and bamboo **sprouts**. Son-sak ate cold rice and mangosteens.

Then Son-sak and his big pet again went clump-clump-clumping their way through the teak forest of Thailand.

—Jennifer Crider

You may not know anyone who rides an elephant, but you might know someone who rides a pony. Maybe you even have a pony.

Trot Along, Pony

Trot along, pony.
  Late in the day,
Down by the meadow
  Is the loveliest way.

The apples are rosy
  And ready to fall.
The branches hang over
  By Grandfather's wall.

But the red sun is sinking
  Away out of sight.
The chickens are settling
  Themselves for the night.

Your stable is waiting
  And supper will come.
So turn again, pony,
  Turn again home.

—*Marion Edey and Dorothy Grider*

> *"And hath made of one blood all nations of men for to dwell on all the face of the earth, and hath determined the times before appointed, and the bounds of their habitation."*
>
> – Acts 17:26

Polder Pals

Andries opened his eyes and stretched. Then he jerked upright. Today was the day he had been looking forward to for weeks. *Thud!* His feet hit the floor. *Bang!* The closet door opened. *Slam!* It shut again. *Thump, thumpety, thump!* He scrambled down the stairs.

Father looked up. "Did you fall out of bed? What's the hurry?" His eyes twinkled.

Andries laughed. He knew Father was teasing him. "I can hardly wait," he said. "I've never been to Alkmaar before, and here I get to go on a **barge**!"

When breakfast was over, he went to watch for the barge. He could hardly believe that he, Andries, was going to live on a canal barge for the next few days. But it was true. His friend Jan lived on a barge all the time. Jan's father delivered flowers, cheeses, and other **goods** all over the Netherlands, and he had invited Andries to visit Jan for several days.

Suddenly Andries spied Jan's barge, still a long way off—beyond the neighbors' cottages. "Here they come!" he called.

The barge moved slowly up the canal toward him. Andries thought he couldn't wait, but finally it **eased** in against the bank. His family waved good-bye as he scrambled up the ladder and over the side of the barge.

"Hi, Andries!" cried Jan. "Are you ready for the ball game?"

"Ball game?" Andries was puzzled.

Jan's father laughed. "Jan is teasing you," he said. "But he is right. You will see a different kind of ball game when we get to Alkmaar—one that you have never seen before."

For the next two days, the barge moved steadily toward Alkmaar, stopping at villages along the way to load big balls of golden cheese stored away in the barge.

To pass the time, Andries and Jan ran races up and down the length of the barge. They played with Jan's dog and his little sister Annetje. Sometimes they simply sat and watched the farms and flower fields and windmills on the level land that stretched away on either side of the canal.

One place they saw two little girls giving their dolls a

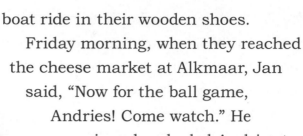

boat ride in their wooden shoes.

Friday morning, when they reached the cheese market at Alkmaar, Jan said, "Now for the ball game, Andries! Come watch." He grinned as he led Andries to where the huge **mounds** of round golden cheeses were stacked on the deck of the barge. As the boys watched, Jan's father grasped a cheese in each hand. Then he threw them to a man waiting on the landing place at the edge of the canal. That man threw the cheeses to a third man who stacked them on a stretcher.

Two by two, the golden balls went flying through the air. Jan's father kept picking up cheeses, throwing them, and turning to get more. The catcher on the landing place never missed a cheese. And from other barges along the canal, other cheeses flew to other catchers on the landing place.

Andries' eyes got wider and wider as he watched the strange ball game.

"This cheese market is famous all over the world," said Jan beside him. "Do you see those men wearing colored hats? They carry the stretchers of cheese to the **warehouse** to be weighed.

"When Father finishes throwing the cheese and it is all weighed, he will go to shore and sell it."

All morning and into the afternoon the ball game went on, until the barge had not a cheese on it. Then Jan's father went to find a buyer for the cheese. He soon came back.

"Well, I sold the cheese," he said, "and now the buyer wants us to deliver it to Amsterdam."

"Oh!" cried Andries. "Will they throw all the cheeses back on the barge?"

"Oh, no," laughed Jan. "That would take too long. Come see."

Men put a wide, long slide from the land down into the barge. A stream of golden cheeses thumped down into the barge. In no time at all the barge was full.

"I wish I lived on a barge and could come to Alkmaar with cheeses," said Andries. "It's fun."

"It is," agreed Jan, "but living on a farm is nice too. Listen, Mother is calling us for supper."

After supper, the boys and Annetje got ready for bed. "Tell us a story before we go to bed. Please, Father," begged Annetje.

"Long, long ago, God created the world," began Jan's

father. "We don't know what everything looked like then, but we do know that when He created the land in this country He made it flat and very low.

"And we know that many, many years ago the North Sea flooded much of the land. It made a large, shallow bay. Under the bay, people knew, was much good land. But no one could use it."

"I know what comes next!" cried Andries. "They built the big dike!"

"Yes. Workers built a long dike all the way across the bay to keep out the North Sea. That dike took twelve years to build, and when they were finished, the bay wasn't a bay anymore—it was a lake. But under the lake was still much good land that no one could use.

"Then workers began to take back the land. They built dikes around large areas and pumped all the water out over the edge of the dike. That made a new piece of land called a polder."

"But Father," said Jan, "the land would be all **soggy**."

"Yes, and that is why we have so many canals in our country. The water can drain into the canals."

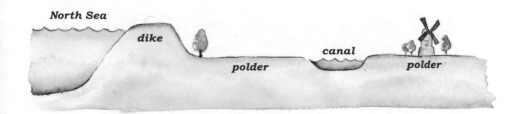

"Wasn't there a big flood one time that broke through the dikes?" Andries wondered.

"Yes, that was not so many years ago," said Jan's mother.

"Only it was not so bad in this part of the country," added Father. "Down in the South the sea was so wild that it broke down the dikes. Hundreds of people were drowned in that storm, and houses were washed away."

"Will it do it again?" asked Annetje, her eyes big.

Her father smiled. "It could happen, I suppose. But with strong dikes and our God in control, we do not need to worry. Now to bed, all of you. We head for Amsterdam tomorrow."

Andries climbed into bed with Jan. He fell asleep to the lap-lapping of water against the side of the barge.

–Jennifer Crider

Do you suppose Jan or Andries had the problem the little boy in this poem had?

Two in Bed

When my brother Tommy
Sleeps in bed with me,
He doubles up
And makes
himself
exactly
like
a
V
And 'cause the bed is not so wide,
A part of him is on my side.

—*A. B. Ross*

Exploring Guatemala

Today we will take a long exploring trip. We will visit Guatemala. Do you know where Guatemala is? South of the United States lies the country of Mexico. In our airplane, we will fly across Mexico. Guatemala is just south of it.

As we fly over the country, you can see mountains, streams, and thick forests below. *This looks like an interesting place*, you decide.

We land 5,000 feet above sea level in Guatemala's largest city—Guatemala City. In the airport you hear people talking all around you in languages you cannot understand. Most Guatemalans speak Spanish, but the many Indians in the country have their own languages too. Before you leave, maybe you will learn a few words of Spanish to use on your friends at home.

You see parks, stores, and **gaily** colored houses that help make much of the city beautiful. But some parts of the city are not so pretty. Many poor people live crowded in broken-down houses; some have no home at all.

While in Guatemala, you will make some new friends. Paco invites us to visit his home. His house is not at all like yours. It is built around a patio—a little yard that you can reach only by going through the house. Every room of the house opens onto the patio.

Because he has company, Paco plans a party. He invites some other children and makes a piñata to fill with candy and nuts. He makes the piñata from yellow, green, and red paper and shapes it like a big bird. Then he hangs it from a wire in the middle of the patio.

When party time comes, Paco's mother blindfolds one of the boys and gives him a long stick. Now you realize that the boy must try to break open the piñata without

being able to see it. The boy swings hard, but misses the piñata. "Two more tries, amigo," calls Paco. On his third swing, the boy hits the piñata, but it does not break.

"Do you want to try, amigo?" Paco asks. He blindfolds you, and you grasp the stick firmly. Swish! Your swing misses completely. But the next time— crack! Nuts and candy scatter over the ground, and the children scramble to pick them up.

"¡Adios!" calls Paco as you leave. "Come again!"

But you want to see more of Guatemala than only the city. "Do you have any farms?" you ask. Of course! Let's visit a banana **plantation**.

To get to the plantation we will take a train down to the coast. There the bananas grow best. We ride for several hours, stopping often at stations along the way.

At the first stop, people come running up to the windows. *What are they doing?* you wonder. Then you see that each one wants to sell something to the passengers. Some sell special Guatemalan gifts to remind you of your trip. Others will sell you something to eat. You can buy a chicken, some eggs, or fruit, and of course, tortillas.

A tortilla is a round, flat kind of bread made of corn flour. You might like to try one plain; or perhaps you would like beans, meat, or cheese rolled up inside.

As the train chugs on, you have plenty of time to look around you. As the train goes near a river, you notice a strange thing. "Look at those houses on stilts!" you exclaim. "Why would anyone build a house that way?"

The man sitting in front of you hears your question and laughs. "In this part of Guatemala, we have a rainy season for several months out of each year. It rains every day and floods the land. Those houses are built on stilts to keep them above the water."

When we finally get off the train, we hire a guide to show us the way and to find horses for us to ride. Off we go to see the plantation. And soon you understand why we ride horses—no car could drive on this narrow road!

When we reach the plantation, we find the owner waiting to show us around. We rattle through the plantation in a little car that rides on railroad tracks. The tracks were built for the trains that carry the bananas.

All around us we see hundreds of banana plants. Each plant has **broad** leaves and one stalk of bananas.

"Look!" you exclaim. "I didn't know bananas grow upside-down!"

"Yes," says the owner. "That is how bananas grow. Can you guess how many bananas grow on one plant?"

"Umm, two hundred?" you guess.

"Not quite that many," says the owner. "From 50 to 100 bananas grow on each plant. They grow in bunches called hands. Each banana in a hand is called—can you guess?"

"A finger?" you ask.

"That's right. Did you notice that we pick the bananas when they are green? That way they reach the stores in other countries without spoiling. We put them on trains that take them to the harbor town. Let's go down to the harbor now. I'll show you what happens next."

The harbor town is a busy place at loading time.

"Here come the bananas!" someone calls. Workers run to meet the train. Each worker grabs a stalk of bananas. He carries it to the fruit boat waiting in the harbor, then hurries back for another load. What a noise and **bustle** as the men rush back and forth, back and forth, until they have taken all the bananas from the train to the boat.

We have time for one more visit before we leave Guatemala. Where shall we go? How about seeing a coffee plantation?

At the coffee plantation, we see a very different kind of plant. Instead of long, broad, light green leaves, the coffee plant has small, **glossy**, dark leaves. Instead of long green and yellow bananas, we see small red berries.

Workers busily pick the ripe coffee berries. Other workers wash them. Finally they go to a machine that breaks them open. Each berry holds two seeds, called beans. We watch workers wash the coffee beans. Then other workers, using long poles, spread them out in the sun to dry. Then the beans go through the machine that sorts out only the largest ones to sell.

Finally the beans are ready to be shipped. Workers pack them into large sacks and load them onto boats. The boats will take them to other countries. There, workers will put the beans into large, hot ovens to roast them. Then, before anyone can have a cup of coffee, the beans need to be ground or made into instant coffee.

Our trip comes to a close. You will have plenty to remember about exploring in Guatemala: trains and tortillas, patios and piñatas, stilts and Spanish, bananas and coffee. Will you want to visit again someday?

—*Jennifer Crider*

Ring
Around
the World

–Annette Wynne

Ring around the world,
　Taking hands together,
All across the temperate
　And the torrid weather.

Past the royal palm trees
　By the ocean sand,
Make a ring around the world,
　Taking each other's hand.

In the valleys, on the hill,
　Over the prairie spaces,
There's a ring around the world
　Made of children's friendly faces.

> *"And hath made of one blood all nations of men for to dwell on all the face of the earth, and hath determined the times before appointed, and the bounds of their habitation."*
>
> – Acts 17:26

The Island Pineapple State

When the United States first became a country in 1776, it had only 13 states. As the years went by, the country grew. By the middle of 1959, there were 49 states. Then a new state became part of the country.

This fiftieth state is not like the others. Instead of being on the continent of North America, it is in the middle of the Pacific Ocean. Instead of being one large area of land, it is made up of eight large islands and over one hundred smaller ones. This state is Hawaii.

Hawaii is a beautiful state. If you would go there, you would see palm trees and colorful flowers, fields of pineapple and sugarcane, volcanoes and **lush** rain forests. You would hear the musical sound of Hawaiian words mixed with the English talk around you.

The Hawaiian language is a soft, musical language. Instead of the 26 letters you use to speak and write English, the Hawaiian alaphabet has 12 letters:

a e h i k l m n o p u w

Would you like to know some Hawaiian words?

aloha	ä lō′ hä	greetings; love
wikiwiki	wē kē wē′ kē	hurry
kaukau	kaů kaů	food
pehea oe	pā hā′ äō′	How are you?
mahalo	mä hä′ lō	thanks
hele mai	hā′ lä mī	come here

Kimo was a Hawaiian boy about your age. He lived on the island of Oahu. Kimo's father worked in the pineapple fields.

One day Father came home and said, "We are getting the fields ready to plant. Today we plowed and got the soil ready. Tomorrow the machine will come to spread the plastic. The next day, Kimo, you will come and help me plant."

Kimo had never before helped to plant pineapples, so he was excited.

Kimo felt very grown-up two days later as he and

his father left home early to go to the pineapple fields. When they reached the large fields, Father handed Kimo a sharp planting tool. "Use this to poke holes in the plastic. I will come behind you and plant the slips."

"Where do the slips come from?" asked Kimo. "They look sort of like small plants."

"They come from pineapple plants. They grow on the stem just below the fruit," said Father. "Sometimes we plant the pineapple crowns and sometimes the suckers. Crowns are the top part of the plant, on top of the fruit. Suckers grow out from the plant roots and come up around the plant."

Kimo shaded his eyes and looked across the fields. Strips of plastic stretched far across the level land. "This is a big job, isn't it, Father?"

"Yes, indeed. We will not finish today."

Kimo began punching holes in the plastic. Father followed, putting the pineapple slips into the holes.

"Why do they put plastic on the fields?" Kimo **inquired.**

"It keeps the soil warm for the plants," answered Father. "And it keeps the weeds from growing. Aren't you glad you don't have to pull all the weeds by hand?"

Kimo nodded. "That would take a long time."

"It would," agreed Father, "and since pineapples take so long to grow, we would have to do it often."

"How long will it be until the pineapples are ready to pick?" asked Kimo.

"Well, we should be picking the first pineapples from these plants in about 20 months," said Father. "That's almost two years from now. Do you remember helping to pick pineapples last year?"

"Oh, yes! We grabbed them by the leaves on top and pulled them off and put them on the belt. It was fun to watch all the pineapples riding the belt up to the truck. I got very tired that day."

"Are you tired now?" asked Father. "Let's take a break. I brought some bananas for a snack."

As they rested, Kimo remarked, "If we worked on a sugar plantation, we wouldn't have to plant the field by hand."

"That's right," Father agreed. "And we wouldn't have to harvest it by hand either."

"What I'd like best about harvesting sugar would be burning off the field. The roar of the fire and the smoke rolling up—that's exciting."

"There's no quicker way to get rid of the leaves and trash, even though it does leave the stalks black. But

they wash them off before they squeeze out the juice."

"Well, it's hard for me to believe that the stalks are so full of juice that they don't burn," said Kimo. "But it sure makes it handy at harvesttime."

"Yes, growing each kind of crop has its easier and harder parts," replied Father. Then he added with a smile, "But it's time for us to stop talking about other people's work and get back to our own."

Kimo and Father went back to work, planting pineapples that would be shipped all over the world for others to enjoy.

–Jennifer Crider

> *"And hath made of one blood all nations of men for to dwell on all the face of the earth, and hath determined the times before appointed, and the bounds of their habitation."*
>
> – Acts 17:26

Trip Behind a Reindeer

Lu Lahli lived in Lapland. She lived across the ocean in the far North, above the Arctic Circle.

Lu Lahli was a nomad. That means she and her people lived in tents and moved about from place to place. When Laplanders needed new pastures for their reindeer, they took down their tents. They rolled them up and loaded them onto sleds along with everything else they owned.

They **hitched** the reindeer to the sleds. Then off they drove to find new pasture.

127

Laplanders could not live without their reindeer. They were the same as horses, cows, sheep, and goats are to other peoples. They gave milk and meat for food. They gave warm fur for clothing, shoes, and gloves. Lu Lahli's people needed reindeer hides to make tents, dishes, and many other things in the home. A reindeer could pull a sled loaded with as much as 300 pounds. It could travel a hundred miles a day.

Laplanders took good care of their reindeer herds. They journeyed along wherever the reindeer needed to go for food.

Lu Lahli was happy she was going on a journey across the mountain to a city by the sea. She had never been to the city and was going this time because she had something to trade.

During the long, dark winter days, Lu Lahli had made many strong shoestrings from reindeer hide. She planned to trade these for gifts for her family.

To get ready, she dressed in her warm fur coat, new gloves, and boots with the red and yellow tops.

In front of their tent, three of the strongest reindeer waited, hitched to sleds. Lu Lahli would ride on the sled behind her own pet reindeer, along with her bundle of shoestrings.

The other sleds were loaded with cups carved from wood, spoons made from reindeer antlers, and beautiful caps, gloves, and boots made from skins. Her father and mother had worked hard to make these during the dark months of winter. A big bundle of fox and wolf skins also found a place on one sled.

Each rider sat flat on his sled with his legs straight out in front.

At last everything was ready. Lu Lahli's father cried, "Time to be off! Time to be off!"

Away flew the first reindeer over the snow. Lu Lahli's sled started next. Her father pulled out last.

"Good-bye! Good-bye!" called Lu Lahli to her mother and the smiling baby brother in his wooden cradle.

Lu Lahli had often traveled on the plains. She knew how to keep her balance on the sled even on a bumpy trail. Nomad children learned how to handle reindeer when they were quite young. Lu Lahli drove **skillfully** with only one line. She threw it to the left to stop her pet and to the right to speed him on again.

But she knew nothing about travel on a mountain trail. They crossed the plain and started up the mountain. Up and up they rode. The reindeer walked now, but they had no trouble pulling the loaded sleds along the narrow, winding trail.

Lu Lahli felt a **thrill** of fear as she looked over the edge of the mountain and saw a straight drop of hundreds of feet. She shut her eyes and turned her head away and prayed that God would keep them safe.

Then she thought about going down the trail on the other side of the mountain. What if the sleds began to go too fast? Suppose they ran into the heels of the reindeer and made them fall down. Suppose the deer turned the wrong way and got too near the edge. Suppose the sleds and all of them were dashed over the mountainside, way, way down there. No one would ever find them.

But then she said to herself, "Father has gone this way many times. He knows how to go safely down the other side."

When at last they reached the top of the mountain, Lu Lahli learned that she was right about her father. Just before the trail began to go down the other side, he called, "Stop." Lu Lahli flipped the rein to the left and her reindeer stopped immediately.

Father unhitched the reindeer from the fronts of the sleds. Then he hitched them to the backs of the sleds with their heads facing downhill.

As her sled started down the trail, Lu Lahli held on tightly with both hands. Her reindeer set his strong feet firmly in the snow and held back the sled so it would not go too fast.

Slowly, carefully, her reindeer eased down the steep trail. Lu Lahli soon saw that she need not be afraid. There was no danger.

At the bottom of the mountain, Father hitched the reindeer to the fronts of the sleds and away they trotted again.

Once more Lu Lahli shut her eyes and prayed. This time she breathed a prayer of thanksgiving.

By nightfall they were not far from the city by the sea. They stopped to spend the night at an inn for travelers. How very strange everything seemed to Lu Lahli!

Her own house was a tent with walls of reindeer hides. The walls of the inn were thick logs. At home three stones on the earth floor served as a stove. The smoke went out a hole in the top of the tent. Here she saw a smooth stone floor and a stone fireplace. The smoke went up a great stone chimney.

Lu Lahli was almost too **weary** to greet her father's friends at the inn. She ate the supper they set before her. But soon she fell fast asleep with her clothes on and her feet toward the blazing fire.

The next morning the travelers went on. Before noon they reached the Lapland city by the sea.

To Lu Lahli it seemed a wonderful place with its pretty streets, its wood and stone houses, and its fine stores.

Her father took her to a store where she traded the shoestrings for gifts. For her mother, Lu Lahli chose a blue handkerchief; for Baby Brother, a pretty toy; and a little doll for herself.

Lu Lahli enjoyed wandering around the store, looking at all the wonderful things. How much she would have to tell her mother when she got home!

Her father traded all the things they had brought for things they needed in their Lapland home. At last he said, "We must go now."

Lu Lahli put her gifts in a safe place on the sled. Then, with her doll in her pocket and joy in her heart, she snuggled in her seat on the sled.

She knew now that the strong, gentle reindeer would carry them safely up and down the mountain. Then one long, fast dash across the plain, and she would be home in their own snug tent.

The city was exciting to visit. But the wandering life of the nomad was the life Lu Lahli loved best.

—Alice Alison Lide

High Home
in the Desert

Blue Cornflower was an Indian girl who lived with her parents, brother, and grandmother in the hot southwestern desert of the United States. She did not live in a tepee or a wigwam or a **hogan**. Her home was made of clay bricks that had been dried in the hot sun. These bricks are called adobe. She lived long ago in a village in what is now the state of New Mexico.

The adobe houses of the village were built against a cliff, one on top of the other, like giant steps. Each house was set farther back than the one below it. The flat roof of one house was the front yard of the one above it. And the roof of that house was the front yard of the house higher up.

133

People who lived in the higher houses reached their homes by **ascending** ladders that leaned against the edge of the next roof.

Many, many years ago when Indian tribes fought each other, the houses on the ground had no doors or windows. That prevented the enemy from getting in. When the people climbed up on the roof, they pulled up the ladder and were safe.

But they had no enemies now. The ladders stayed in place. Blue Cornflower and her little brother could go up and down the ladders whenever they pleased.

In the cool mornings, they played on the desert sands in front of the village or helped in the field. In the hot afternoons, they found quiet things to do in the shade of their own adobe home. Their house was

the highest in the whole village. That meant they had to climb more ladders than anyone else. But they didn't mind that, because when they got home they could see for miles around. They could look down on all the neighbors below them.

Now they heard their mother ascending the ladder from the roof below. She had one, two, three ladders to reach home from the ground.

She balanced a pottery jar of fresh water on her head. No water splashed out of the jar, even when she ascended the ladders.

The children ran to meet her, their black eyes shining.

"I know what you are going to make," cried Blue Cornflower. "You are going to grind corn and make bread for supper."

"And it will have honey in it," added Little Brother.

"Yes, but I will need a girl to grind the corn first."

"That will be me," said Blue Cornflower. Grinding the dried grains of corn between two stones was her job. It was hard work because the top stone was so heavy.

Round and round she turned the stone until she had a pile of soft, fine cornmeal. Blue Cornflower carried it to the fireplace in the corner of the adobe house. There her mother stirred water and honey into it to make a soft, thin dough. She also stirred in dried desert flowers.

Mother spread the dough over a hot stone in the

fireplace. The thin dough on the stone baked very quickly. Blue Cornflower and her brother were glad when it was ready to eat.

Mother said they could each eat one piece before supper. Blue Cornflower balanced the hot bread on her open hand and took half of it to Grandmother who was making a pottery bowl to sell.

Grandmother had brought clay from a mountain far away. She had rubbed the clay between stones until it was as fine as flour. Then she mixed it with water into a smooth clay. She rolled the clay into a long, smooth rope.

Next she curled the rope in a circle around and around, higher and higher, into the shape of a jar. Then she took a small flat stone and rubbed the jar inside and out. With wet hands she smoothed the clay until it was as slick as glass.

After the jar dried in the sun, Grandmother would fire it in a hot oven. The jars and bowls that Grandmother painted with bright colors were the ones Blue Cornflower liked best. She was learning to make pottery too, but it would be a long time before she could do as fine and beautiful work as Grandmother did.

Cool evening breezes began to stir before the children saw their father coming home. He had worked all day on their farm on the plain. Corn, beans, cotton, and squash grew fast in the hot sunshine. He climbed one ladder, two ladders, and finally up the last ladder. Blue Cornflower thought the best time of the day was when Father got home.

After supper the family sat in front of their house and watched the purple shadows creep across the hot golden sands. She and Little Brother counted the stars as they came out one by one.

At bedtime a mat and a blanket were all Blue Cornflower and Little Brother needed. They drifted off to sleep listening to the quiet voices of Father and Mother and Grandmother talking over the things that had happened that day.

—Ann Nolan Clark

No matter where in the world children may
live, we know Jesus loves them. Years ago,
children sang this poem as a song.

The World's Children

The cunning papoose in the wigwam that lives,
Whose life is so happy and free—
Is my Indian brother,
And Jesus loves him, just as He loves
    you and me.

Chorus *(Repeat after each verse.)*
    The world's children for Jesus,
    The world's children for Jesus,
    The world's children for Jesus,
    Who loves them—who loves every one.

The Eskimo babies are wrapped all in fur;
They live in the north country
Where cold winds blow,
And Jesus loves them, just as He loves
    you and me.

The Japanese babies with shining dark eyes
Live on a green isle in the sea—
Too many to count.
And Jesus loves them, just as He loves
    you and me.

The little brown babies who roll in the sand
In a country far over the sea
Are my African brothers,
And Jesus loves them, just as He loves
    you and me.

And all the dear babies wherever they grow—
So cunning, so precious, so wee—
Are God's darling children,
And Jesus loves them, just as He loves
    you and me.

–Author Unknown

> *"Their idols are silver and gold,*
> *the work of men's hands."*
>
> – Psalm 115:4

A Wooden God or the God of Heaven?

Part 1

Chan's black eyes opened wide. He was much surprised and half scared. Had the missionary really said that? He had never heard such a thing before.

"An idol is nothing." The missionary said it again. "If it is made of wood, it is just like any other piece of wood that you burn in your stove.

"If it is made of brass, it can do no more than the bell that calls you to school. If it is made of stone, it can do no more than the stone you throw at a dog.

"Wood cannot make it rain. Brass cannot make your crops grow. Stone cannot bring you bad luck. Idols cannot see what you do or hear what you say.

"Only the God of Heaven can do that. He knows what we need. He loves us and wants us to love Him. He takes care of children and hears when they pray to Him."

Chan and all the children sat very still. They looked at the missionary teacher. They looked at each other. But no one said a word.

Then the missionary began telling the story of an idol from the book of the God of Heaven. But Chan did not hear the story. He was thinking of the god in his home. The god was made of wood. It was fat and ugly. The missionary said it was an idol!

His mother kept a candle burning in front of it day and night. "We must keep the candle burning or the god will become angry," she said.

Every morning the family bowed to the wooden god with their faces to the floor. As long as Chan could remember, his mother had told him, "Do not say anything bad about our god. It will hear you and become angry. Then it will bring some evil on us."

On the way home from the mission school, Chan thought and thought about what the missionary had said.

How wonderful it would be if he did not need to be afraid of the wooden god! How wonderful it would be to have a god who loved you!

He thought of how their god sat on the shelf with its

wooden eyes staring straight ahead. Did it really know the candle was burning in front of it? Could it really hear with its wooden ears? Could it really bring evil upon you if you said something bad about it?

His family did not need any bad luck. His father was lame. He worked in a shoe factory and did a good job. But he could not work very fast. So he did not make much money.

He was always afraid his job would be given to a man who could work faster than he.

Chan's mother said, "We must keep the candle burning in front of the god so that you do not lose your job."

How wonderful it would be to have a god who would help you instead of sending bad luck!

Suddenly, as he was going home, Chan said right out loud, "I am going to find out for myself if our god can see and hear and bring evil on us. I will do something that will tell me if it can see. I will do something that will tell me if that god can hear. I will do something that will tell me if it can do anything."

Chan entered the quiet and empty house. He knew his mother had gone to the market. Every afternoon she went there to buy fresh food for supper.

Chan went in and looked at the idol. It was on the shelf where it always sat. Its wooden eyes stared straight ahead at nothing.

The boy's heart began to beat faster. He was afraid. But he went up to the idol and blew out the candle!

He stepped back, his eyes wide with fear over what he had done. But nothing happened. The wooden god kept staring straight ahead with its wooden eyes. Even when the smoke from the **wick** blew into its face, it did not move.

Chan stood still for a long minute. Then he whispered, "You are nothing!"

He waited, breathing hard. All was quiet.

He took a deep breath and said out loud, "You are nothing but wood, and you are ugly!"

Then he said as loud as he could, "Send some bad luck if you can. I do not think you can do anything!"

A little later when he heard his mother's voice in the street, he slipped out the back door into the garden. Soon he heard her sharp cry of fear, and he knew she had seen the blown-out candle.

Chan stood very still under the trees. What had he done? Maybe he had brought evil on his family. Maybe now his father would lose his job!

Then he thought about the God of Heaven. The missionary had said He was a God who heard and helped when people prayed to Him.

"God of Heaven," whispered Chan, "please keep my family from evil. And help me to know for sure about idols."

Chan stayed outside until he saw his father limping home from work. Then he went in, because he knew supper would be ready.

His mother looked worried, though she had lighted the candle again in front of the wooden god.

As soon as they began eating, she said, "Something made the candle go out. The wind must have blown it out. But it was not windy today. I cannot think why it was not burning when I got home from market. Do you think we will have bad luck now?"

"Well, we have had no bad luck yet," said Father. "This supper is extra good. Where did you get the chicken? We have not had chicken for a long time."

"I got it free. Its leg was broken," said Mother. "No one would buy it. The market man gave it to me for nothing."

"That was *good* luck!" said Chan in surprise. He thought of his prayer to the God of Heaven and suddenly felt very happy. Had the God of Heaven really answered his prayer?

"I must have gotten the chicken before the candle went out," said his mother. But Chan knew that was not so.

"The bad luck may come tomorrow," said Father. "Another man came today. He wants my job. He says he can work faster than I. Tomorrow they are going to try him out. If he works faster than I, they will give him my job."

"It is because the candle went out," cried Mother. "The god is angry! It is bringing evil upon us! Let us put two candles in front of it. Maybe it will not be angry anymore."

"No," said Father. "Another candle will cost money. And no bad luck has come yet. If the god knows anything, he knows you did not try to make the candle go out. Let's wait and see what happens tomorrow."

—Ruth K. Hobbs

> *"They have mouths, but they speak not:*
> *eyes have they, but they see not."*
>
> – Psalm 115:5

A Wooden God or the God of Heaven?

Part 2

The next morning a loud **shriek** from his mother woke Chan. He sat straight up in bed.

"The god! Our god! It is gone! What could have become of it?" he heard his mother cry.

Chan's eyes grew round with fear. But then he whispered, "God of Heaven, help me now!"

He jumped out and looked under his bed. Then he kneeled down as the missionary did at school. "God of Heaven," he prayed, "show me if idols are anything. Show me if You are real. Show me if You can hear me and keep evil from my family for what I have done. Show

146

me if You can keep my father from losing his job."

Chan dressed and went out to his mother. She was crying. He watched his father walking around looking behind this and under that. He did not find the wooden god. "Someone must have come in the night and stolen it," he said.

Chan took a deep breath. He said, "Maybe it ran away because the candle went out."

His mother stopped crying and looked at him. His father stopped walking around the room and looked at him.

"Do not be foolish," said his father. "The god could not run away."

"Do not be foolish," said his mother. "The god could not do such a thing."

"Why not?" asked Chan.

"Because . . ." began his father. Then he stopped.

"Because—well, just because," said his mother.

"Why didn't it do something if someone came and stole it? Can't a god keep itself safe from a thief?"

Mother looked at Father and Father looked at Mother. They did not say anything.

Then Chan said, "At the mission school, the teacher told us that our gods are nothing. They are not alive. They cannot help us or harm us. He said we should worship the God of Heaven who lives and who loves us. The God of Heaven does not bring evil on His people. He helps them when they need help."

Mother and Father just looked at Chan. They had never heard such a thing.

Then Chan said, "I have something I must tell you. I wanted to discover if the god could see, so I blew out the candle. I wanted to discover if it could hear. I told the god it was ugly. I told it I did not believe it could bring us bad luck.

"And then we had the good chicken for supper! So it did not bring us bad luck. It couldn't, because it did not see me or hear me say those things."

Chan took another deep breath. "I must tell you something else. I wanted to discover if idols can do anything. So last night I took the idol. I put it on its face under my bed. I wanted to see if it knew enough to get up in the morning. I wanted to see if it could come out from under my bed. But it is still there. Do you think it will ever come out by itself?"

Mother gave a loud shriek. She jumped up and started for Chan's room.

"Stop!" said Father. "Do not get it. Let it come out by itself if it can. Let it stay there till I come home from work today.

"I, too, would like to find out if that wooden god can bring evil on us. If I lose my job today, then we will know the idol brought bad luck because of what Chan did."

"I have asked the God of Heaven not to let that man get your job," said Chan.

"It is good," said Father. "I want to find out about this God of Heaven. I want to find out if He can keep that man from taking my job. We will find out today."

Father went to work and Chan went to school.

Never had a day been so long. Chan could think of nothing but the idol under his bed and Father's job.

Had Mother put the wooden god back on its shelf? Would the new man work faster than Father and get his job? Or had the God of Heaven heard his prayer? Was He able to help?

When Chan got home, his mother was there. She had not gone to the market. She looked sad and worried, but she said nothing about what Chan had done.

At last Father came limping home.

"Oh, Father," cried Chan. "Did that man come? Could he work faster than you? Did they give him your job?"

"Yes, the new man came. He could work faster than I. They gave him my job," said Father.

Mother threw up her hands and began to cry loudly, "I told you the god would be angry and send evil on us. Now you have no work! What will become of us? Oh, what are we going to do?"

Chan looked at his father. His father did not look worried. In fact, he was smiling.

Then he said, "Yes, the new man could work faster

than I, so they gave him my job. But he did not know as much about making shoes as I. He could not work as well as I. They gave me other work that needs to be done perfectly. I do not need to work fast at the new job as long as I do it perfectly. And they will pay me more."

Mother stopped crying before Father had finished talking. Now she said, "Chan, go get that god that can't even crawl out from under a bed. Let us put it in the fire."

"Yes," agreed Father. "But first let us get down on our knees and thank the God of Heaven, who can hear, and who answers the prayer of even a boy."

—Ruth K. Hobbs

> *"They have ears, but they hear not: noses have they, but they smell not."*
>
> – Psalm 115:6

The Drowned Idols

Part 1

A hundred years ago, two small boys padded along a dusty road in India. They were going home to the little mud hut where they lived with their parents and little sister.

As they came within sight of their home, Paras said, "I wonder why Father is home from work this time of day. See, the oxcart is there at the house."

"Something must be wrong," replied Agnew, the younger of the brothers. "Let's hurry!"

As they entered the neat little hut, they heard their father saying, "We have not had enough rain. No rain means no rice crop. No rice crop means no work for me.

No job means no money. No money means no food. I don't know what will become of us."

Father looked worried. Mother looked worried. Even Baby Sister sat on Mother's lap with no smile on her sweet brown face.

Then Paras said, "Maybe we should pray."

"I have thought of that," said Father, "but . . ." He stopped.

"Yes," said Mother. "We must pray because we can do nothing else."

She set the baby on the floor. She brought out five small stone idols and set them in a row.

Then Father, Mother, Paras, and Agnew knelt on the mud floor in front of them. They bowed their heads to the floor on their folded hands. Father **earnestly** asked the idols to send them rain or food, or **provide** a new job for him.

The next day, they prayed to the idols again. But it did not rain.

Father spent the whole day in the city looking for work, but he found no job. He came home weary and discouraged.

That evening there was not enough rice to take away their hunger. Paras and Agnew went to bed feeling empty and worried. From their sleeping mats, they saw their parents kneeling before the row of idols. They heard their whispered prayers for food and work.

The next morning the oxcart stood at the door.

"What are you doing, Father?" asked Paras.

"I am loading some of our **possessions** to sell. We need money to buy rice. Then we must move away from here."

"I don't want to move!" cried Paras. "This is our home! Where will we go?"

"I don't know where we will go; but we must leave here or we will starve."

"I don't want to move either," said Agnew. "While you are gone I am going to pray to our gods again. I will pray that you will get a lot of money for the things you are selling."

"I will pray too," said Paras. "But I am going to ask the gods to give you work so that we don't have to move."

"And I will pray too," said Mother. "But I will pray for food. Surely the gods can see that we need food."

"All right," said Father. "You may pray, but I am beginning to wonder if those gods . . ." Father started the oxen without finishing his sentence.

Mother, Paras, and Agnew knelt once more before the row of stone gods. Again they earnestly begged for food and for money from the sale of their possessions. They asked for a job for Father.

Before noon, Father returned weary and worried. He had not gotten much money for the things he had taken to sell. "No one else has money either," he said. "But I did get enough to buy some rice. Please cook some, Mother. We all are hungry. While you do that, I will load the rest of the things. Then we must be on our way."

"Oh, Father, must we go?" cried Paras.

And Agnew said, "But we prayed! Maybe the gods will find you a job tomorrow."

Father said nothing. He just began to roll up their sleeping mats.

After they had each eaten a small bowl of rice, they helped take out the rest of their possessions. It did not take long to empty the little mud hut.

Father pulled the door shut, and the oxen began to move out onto the hot, dusty road. Mother sat on top of the load holding the baby. Father and the boys walked on either side.

"Where are we going?" Paras and Agnew asked again and again as the burning sun rose higher and higher.

Mother only shook her head as she looked down on the two weary little fellows trudging along beside the slow oxen.

But Father just kept walking along without answering.

Whenever they met someone on the road, Father asked if they knew where he could find work. No one knew.

At each village they passed, Father asked if anyone had work for him. No one did.

Toward evening, Father led the oxen off the road and through a field to the river. There on the bank they made ready to spend the night.

Father unhitched the oxen and led them to the river

to drink. He tied them where they could eat grass.

All of them washed their weary bodies in the cool water. Then Mother pulled the cooking pot from the cart and started a small fire. A little cooked rice was all they had for supper.

Paras and Agnew pulled out the sleeping mats and spread them under the trees. Father took the stone gods from the cart and set them in a row on the riverbank. Before they lay down to sleep, they asked the gods very earnestly to help them and give them food.

—Aunt Lina

> *"They have hands, but they handle not: feet have they, but they walk not: neither speak they through their throat."*
>
> – Psalm 115:7

The Drowned Idols

Part 2

In the morning, Father watered the oxen and hitched them to the cart. Paras and Agnew rolled up the sleeping mats and stored them in the cart while Mother cooked the last of the rice.

"Where are we going now?" asked Paras.

"We will just keep going," said Father. "But I have one more thing to do before we leave. All of you come with me."

Mother, with the baby and the two boys, followed Father. There on the riverbank sat the five stone gods in a row. Father stood in front of them and said in a loud voice, "You gods! You have not helped us at all. We have prayed to you and you have done nothing! Now I will give you one more chance. Make it rain! Give us food! Tell me where I can find work! Do these things right now! Do just *one* of them, if you can! Do something or I will drown you in the river!"

Mother gasped. Paras and Agnew watched with wide, frightened eyes. Even Father looked afraid as he stood and waited.

Nothing happened.

Then Father stepped forward. He grasped the first god by its round, stone head and flung it far out over the water. It hit with a splash and sank.

Father picked up the next one and the next one. As fast as he could, he **slung** them into the slow flowing river. *Splash! Splash! Splash! Splash!*

"We will go now," said Father quietly.

Back to the waiting oxen they went. Father held the baby while Mother climbed on top of the load. Then he handed up the little girl and picked up his walking staff. Off they started.

Paras and Agnew did not talk for a long time.

After traveling for several hours, they came to a pond with trees around it. A number of men were resting in the shade with their loaded donkeys.

"We will stop here and rest the oxen and let them drink," said Father. "These men might know where I can find work."

While the oxen drank, Father talked to the men.

"Yes, we heard of a place where missionaries are building a road. They have come across the ocean to tell us about their God. They want to help our people in any way they can," said one.

"We have heard they are giving work to as many people as possible. You could go there and ask," said another.

Father learned that the road-building project was more than five miles away, down another road. He came back to the cart with a smile in his tired eyes.

"I don't know what missionaries are, but it doesn't matter. If they will give me a job, I don't care if they are monkeys. Come, boys, we must go and inquire about this. And we must hurry. Mother and Baby Sister will stay here in the shade and rest. We will come back as soon as we find out something."

Mother sat in the shade by the pond. She waited and waited, but Father and the boys did not come. The afternoon wore away and still they did not come. The baby cried with hunger. Mother cried in sadness and **discouragement.** Finally they both fell asleep.

ॐ　　ॐ　　ॐ　　ॐ　　ॐ

"Mother! Mother! Look! Look! See what we have brought!" It was Paras and Agnew shaking her awake.

And there was Father with a new, glad look in his eyes. "They gave us work as soon as we got there. That is why we are so late," he said.

"Oh, Mother," cried Paras. "You should see them! They have such strange reddish-white faces and hair like rice straw."

"But they are so kind," put in Agnew. "They gave us something to eat as soon as we got there. They said people can't work if they are hungry. And they gave us work. Father can use the oxcart to haul logs, and Paras and I can carry earth in baskets and dump it where they need it!"

Then Father explained. "The missionaries are making a road and they are going to build—they called it a church—but I think it is a sort of temple for their God. We will have work until the road and the temple are finished. When I told them how we had to leave our home because the rice crop failed, they said their God had brought us to them. They said He loves everyone and helps those who love Him."

"And see, Mother, the missionaries paid us already for the work we did today, and we bought food!" cried Paras.

"Just see. We have enough for supper and for breakfast and dinner tomorrow too!" cried Agnew. The boys danced around their mother and little sister in excitement.

Mother was so happy and surprised she could hardly talk. Finally she said, "But what kind of people are these? What is a missionary? If they came from across the ocean, maybe they are the **foreign** devils our priests warned us about."

Father laughed. It was the first time the boys had heard their father laugh for a long, long time.

"Our priests? We have no priests, Mother. They are priests of the **worthless** gods lying on the bottom of the river. I know nothing about the missionaries' God. But He must be better than the ones we have been praying to for so long.

"Let us eat supper. Then we must load our possessions. We must move closer to where the road is being built. I mean to ask questions and learn all I can about the God these missionaries are serving. I am sure He is not a god you can drown in a river."

—Aunt Lina

> *"They that make them are like unto them; so is every one that trusteth in them."*
>
> – Psalm 115:8

My God Against Yours

21. And Elijah came unto all the people, and said, How long halt ye between two opinions? if the LORD be God, follow him: but if Baal, then follow him. And the people answered him not a word.

22. Then said Elijah unto the people, I, even I only, remain a prophet of the LORD; but Baal's prophets are four hundred and fifty men.

23. Let them therefore give us two bullocks; and let them choose one bullock for themselves, and cut it in pieces, and lay it on wood, and put no fire under: and I will **dress** the other bullock, and lay it on wood, and put no fire under:

24. And call ye on the name of your gods, and I will call on the name of the LORD: and the God that answereth by fire, let him be God. And all the people answered and said, It is well spoken.

26. And they took the bullock which was given them, and they dressed it, and called on the name of Baal from morning even until noon, saying, O Baal, hear us. But there was no voice, nor any that answered. And they leaped upon the altar which was made.

28. And they cried aloud, and cut themselves after their manner with knives and lancets, till the blood **gushed** out upon them.

31. And Elijah took twelve stones . . .

32. And with the stones he built an altar in the name of the LORD: and he made a **trench** about the altar, as great as would contain two measures of seed.

33. And he put the wood in order, and cut the bullock in pieces, and laid him on the wood, and said, Fill four barrels with water, and pour it on the burnt sacrifice, and on the wood.

34. And he said, Do it the second time. And they did it the second time. And he said, Do it the third time. And they did it the third time.

35. And the water ran round about the altar; and he filled the trench also with water.

36. And it came to pass at the time of the offering of the evening sacrifice, that Elijah the prophet came near, and said, LORD God of Abraham, Isaac, and of Israel, let it be known this day that thou art God in Israel, and that I am thy servant, and that I have done all these things at thy word.

38. Then the fire of the LORD fell, and **consumed** the burnt sacrifice, and the wood, and the stones, and the dust, and licked up the water that was in the trench.

39. And when all the people saw it, they fell on their faces: and they said, The LORD, he is the God; the LORD, he is the God.

– 1 Kings 18:21-24, 28, 31-36, 38, 39

God and Idols

Our God is in the heavens:
   He hath done whatsoever he hath pleased.

Their idols are silver and gold,
   The work of men's hands.
They have mouths, but they speak not:
   Eyes have they, but they see not:
They have ears, but they hear not:
   Noses have they, but they smell not:
They have hands, but they handle not:
   Feet have they, but they walk not:
   Neither speak they through their throat.
They that make them are like unto them;
   So is every one that trusteth in them.

O Israel, trust thou in the Lord:
   He is their help and their shield.
O house of Aaron, trust in the Lord:
   He is their help and their shield.
Ye that fear the Lord, trust in the Lord:
   He is their help and their shield.

–Psalm 115:3-11

> *"If ye have faith ... ye shall say unto this mountain, Be thou removed, and be thou cast into the sea; it shall be done."*
>
> – Matthew 21:21

Be Thou Removed

Twenty little girls had finished supper in an orphanage in India. Now they sat on the floor **clustered** around the missionary. Sister Frances always read from the Bible and prayed with them before bedtime.

"Girls, listen to these words of Jesus: 'Verily I say unto you, If ye have faith, and doubt not ... ye shall say unto this mountain, Be thou removed, and be thou cast into the sea; it shall be done. And all things, whatsoever ye shall ask in prayer, believing, ye shall receive.'"

Mona raised her hand. "Does that mean *our* mountain? If we tell it to be removed and cast into the sea, will God remove it like it says in that verse?"

All the orphans knew what Mona meant by "our" mountain. The orphanage was built on the side of a mountain above the sea. "Our" mountain was really only a small peak on the top. But it rose so steeply west of the building that the sun disappeared behind it early in the afternoon. The orphanage lay in its cold shadow for hours before the day was actually over.

Warmth from the sun all afternoon would mean so much to the orphanage. But there stood the mountain.

Sister Frances looked at Mona.

"Could God move our mountain, Sister Frances?" asked the little girl again. "Isn't that what Jesus said in that verse?"

"Yes, that is what Jesus said, and God certainly can move our mountain," the missionary **assured** her.

"Well then, let's all pray that He will," cried the girls. "Wouldn't it be wonderful if we had sunshine all day long?"

"Indeed it would," agreed Sister Frances **fervently**. "But we do not know if it is God's will for the mountain to be removed. We will ask Him to remove the mountain only if it is His will. Then we must be satisfied with what He decides."

So all the girls prayed and Sister Frances prayed.

"Now it is bedtime, girls," said the teacher.

Then Mona said, "Wait. Jesus said we must *tell* the mountain to be removed. Come, girls, we must tell it like it says in the verse." Mona went to the west window and opened it. The other girls clustered around her. Together they shouted out to the black wall of the mountain, "Be thou removed, and be thou cast into the sea!"

Then they closed the window and went off to bed wondering if the mountain would be gone in the morning.

৵   ৵   ৵   ৵   ৵

"Sister Frances, the mountain is still there," announced the girls at breakfast the next morning.

"Yes, I noticed," replied the missionary with a smile. "Does the verse say how soon God would remove the mountain?"

"No, it doesn't. We must not doubt, but keep on praying. We must keep on telling it to move until it does," the girls decided.

"If it is God's will," reminded Sister Frances.

"Yes, if it is His will," agreed all the girls.

That day the girls decided to help answer their prayer. They took buckets up the mountain and filled them with stones and dirt. Then they carried them down and emptied them over the high bank below the orphanage. They worked at this for about an hour and came in hot, dirty, and **exhausted**.

"Sister Frances, all that work didn't help a bit," they reported. "God will have to remove the mountain all by Himself."

So they stopped trying to move the mountain. But they kept praying fervently every evening and morning. And every night they clustered around the west window and called out to the mountain, "Be thou removed, and be thou cast into the sea."

᠎ ᠎ ᠎ ᠎ ᠎

Then came the excitement of helping Sister Frances prepare to leave for a missionary **conference** at Bombay. She would be gone for almost a month. As they waved good-bye, they reminded her to keep praying about the mountain.

A few days after she left, there came a knock on the door of the orphanage. The man who stood there said, "I have come from the British government. The sea has been washing away the land on the other side of the mountain. A lot of the shore has washed away. We would like your permission to level off the mountain behind your orphanage and use the rocks to fill in the land and build up the shoreline. Would you give us permission to do that?"

It did not take long for permission to be given and the necessary papers signed.

In a few days bulldozers arrived. Then the delighted girls heard blasting and the drone of huge trucks and earthmoving machines.

Day after day, long lines of trucks inched down the

mountain carrying away tons of rocks and earth. Little by little the top of the mountain disappeared.

Mona and her friends no longer prayed for the mountain to be removed, for they could see God answering their prayer every day. Now they just fervently thanked Him over and over.

But in the evening after prayer time, they could not **resist** opening the window and shouting, "Be thou removed, and be thou cast into the sea!"

They could hardly wait until Sister Frances came back. At the same time, they hoped she would not come before the mountain really was gone.

The afternoon she arrived at the train station, they all went to meet her. After the glad greetings were over, Mona said, "We have a surprise, so you must be blindfolded until we reach home."

Of course, Sister Frances could not imagine what the surprise was. At the orphanage they led her to the west window and removed the blindfold. Sister Frances blinked in astonishment in the warm sunshine.

"Why—why—where . . . the mountain!" she gasped. "It's gone!" The girls laughed joyously. They clustered around her, all talking at once, trying to tell everything that had happened.

"We told the mountain to leave and be cast into the sea and that's exactly what happened," said one.

"Aren't you glad it was God's will?" said another.

"Now we get the warm sunshine all afternoon," said a third.

Sister Frances was almost too astonished to say a word.

That evening at devotions, Mona asked, "Sister Frances, would you please read that verse again?"

So the missionary read, "'Verily I say unto you, If ye have faith, and doubt not . . . ye shall say unto this mountain, Be thou removed, and be thou cast into the sea; it shall be done. And all things, whatsoever ye shall ask in prayer, believing, ye shall receive.'"

That night no one talked to the mountain because it had truly been cast into the sea.

—adapted

The person in this poem is glad for a hill.
She wouldn't want to get rid of her hill.

Afternoon on a Hill

I will be the gladdest thing
   Under the sun!
I will touch a hundred flowers
   And not pick one.

I will look at cliffs and clouds
   With quiet eyes,
Watch the wind blow down the grass,
   And the grass rise.

And when the lights begin to show
   Up from the town,
I will mark which must be mine,
   And then start down!

              –Edna St. Vincent Millay

> *"Wise men lay up knowledge."*
>
> – Proverbs 10:14

The Flying Whale

Johnny Liklak was an Eskimo boy. He had round brown cheeks, twinkling black eyes, and a smiling face.

Johnny lived in the far North in an Eskimo village called Arnak.

When anyone says "Eskimo village," most of us think of round **igloos** made of snow. But igloos are not the regular homes of most Eskimos.

In Arnak, black sheds showed above the snow fields. Little black stovepipes rose from the roofs.

Most of the time, the Eskimos lived in wooden houses or huts made of **sod**. Only on their long hunting trips did they cut hard blocks of snow and make igloos for themselves.

The long roof of the trade store rose high above the other buildings. Arnak was a trading station where the Eskimo hunters brought many sled loads of fox, wolf, bear, and seal skins. They also brought whalebone and walrus **ivory** to the little store.

These they traded with the storekeeper for cloth, knives, and shining pots and pans.

Not far from the store stood the low schoolhouse. There Miss True taught the boys and girls.

> *Another Eskimo Game*
>
> ## Nuglugagtug
>
> *A piece of bone with a hole in it is hung from the ceiling. The players try to be the first to poke their stick through the hole.*

One day the children hurried to school—all but Johnny Liklak. He came last.

Johnny loved his teacher, but he did not like school. He liked much better to pretend he was a walrus hunter out on the edge of the sea ice. He liked much better to play a game with the deerskin ball filled with sand.

Today he went slowly to his bench and opened his book. Reading seemed very hard. He thought, *What is the use of learning to read this print? It does not help me in any way. It does not tell me how to shoot walrus or hunt the polar bear or catch the seal.*

Suddenly he heard a faint humming far away. It grew louder and louder until it became a great buzzing above the schoolhouse. Johnny jumped to his feet in fear.

The other children jumped up too. The buzzing noise

grew into a roar. The children had never heard anything like it.

Miss True and the children rushed out the door. There overhead buzzed a huge noisy thing. It had stiff wings.

"It's a duck, the biggest duck in the world!" cried a little girl.

"No, no!" shouted Johnny. "It is a whale, a big whale with wings flying in the sky."

"Oh, it's an airplane!" cried Miss True. "Look, children, look! It is a big beautiful airplane. It will not harm you.

"I wonder if the pilot is in trouble. Maybe he is nearly out of gasoline. We have no gasoline in Arnak."

Round and round circled the airplane. But as there was no landing field, the pilot could not come to the ground.

Suddenly the plane swooped low over the schoolhouse and back up again. Johnny's sharp eyes saw something floating down from the sky. He ran and picked it up and gave it to Miss True.

It was a note which read, "Where am I? What village is this?"

Swiftly Miss True began to run to and fro, drawing lines in the snow with a piece of whalebone. But she knew the lines could not be read from the airplane. So she cried, "Stand on the lines, children. Be quick!"

The children stood close together on the lines, but there were not enough **pupils** to fill them. What could be done?

"Run, Johnny, and get everyone in the village," Miss True cried.

Johnny ran to the store and the houses, shouting for everyone to come. Soon many men and women came streaming down the snow path to the schoolhouse.

And all the time the flying whale circled around and around over them.

In a few moments the lines had been filled with people standing side by side.

As Johnny looked, a great surprise came over him. Why, these people standing on the lines in the snow spelled the word *A-R-N-A-K!*

Here was the name of his village in letters twelve feet high. Words did not need to be printed on paper. You could write on anything. The man in the flying whale could see the letters in the snow. But what if he could not read?

But of course he could read. Again he circled and swooped toward the school. Down came another note. This one read, "Which direction is Netka from here?"

Miss True raced to another place in the snow and printed the word *S-O-U-T-H*. Then the people quickly went and stood on those lines.

The pilot waved his hand and headed toward the south.

After the airplane had gone, the children went back into the schoolhouse. They were so excited they could hardly get back to work. But all the time Johnny Liklak was thinking about the letters in the snow.

So that is what printing does! When people cannot hear you talk, print tells them things they want to know. If you know how to read, you can learn things other people want to tell you. You could read things written by people you never saw! You would find out what people wrote before you were born! There are many, many more things to read in books than could ever be printed in the snow for one person to read!

It is as wonderful for me to read print in my reading book as it is for that airplane man to read those letters in the snow!

The next week the schoolchildren heard the same far-off humming. Then they heard the same buzzing. Again the airplane roared over the school. Everyone rushed out.

The flying whale circled and swooped almost to the ground. Down dropped a package. All the children ran for it, but Johnny got to it first.

In the package were ten pounds of candy. And there was a note which read, "For the children who printed the signs. Thank you for your help. We reached Netka before our gasoline ran out. You saved our lives."

Miss True cried, "Ten pounds of candy, children! What a feast we shall have today! There is enough for everyone in the village."

As he ate the good candy, Johnny Liklak said to himself, "Going to school and learning to read is fine. Yes, indeed, it is fine!"

—*Alice Alison Lide*

A Sledding Song

Sing a song of winter,
　Of frosty clouds in air!
Sing a song of snowflakes
　Falling everywhere.

　　　Sing a song of winter!
　　　　Sing a song of sleds!
　　　Sing a song of tumbling
　　　　Over heels and heads.

Up and down a hillside
　When the moon is bright,
Sledding is a tip-top
　Wintertime delight.

—Norman C. Schlichter

> *"Yet have I not seen the righteous forsaken,*
> *nor his seed begging bread."*
> – Psalm 37:25

Bread Through
the Blizzard

"Now we will pray the Lord's Prayer," said Mother.

Joel knelt down at his little stool. The stool was a piece of log that Father had cut just the right size for Joel. Mother had **attached** a rabbit skin to the top to make it soft and warm.

Now Joel knelt with his hands folded and head bowed on the rabbit skin and prayed, "'Our Father which art in heaven ... Give us this day our daily bread ...'"

Every morning they prayed this prayer. Yesterday morning and this morning were different, though, because Mother led family worship. It was different without Father.

The winter out West for these **settlers** had been long and hard. As soon as the settlers had cleared one snow off the roads, another **blizzard** roared in. For weeks and weeks it had not been safe for Father to start after supplies. Town was twenty miles away. In the horse and wagon, it would take all day even with an early start.

Their supplies were almost **exhausted**. True, they had milk from the cow. But they had no meat, beans, potatoes, flour, salt, or sugar. Only a little **meal** remained. Johnnycake and cornmeal mush, cornmeal mush and johnnycake—that is what they had been eating for several days.

On Monday, Father had seen the stars shining in the early morning sky. He had done the chores as quickly as he could. Then before sunup, he had started with the horse and wagon for the town, twenty miles across the plain.

Joel dressed warmly and played outside. It was the first he had played in the sun for many weeks. The air was so clear he could see the smoke from their nearest neighbor's place, two miles away.

He thought of all the good things Father would bring from town. At last they would have something to eat besides mush and johnnycake.

But by dinnertime, the sun looked **hazy**. In the afternoon, the sky turned gray. By evening, a few fine snowflakes began sifting down. And they knew another blizzard was on the way.

Mother did the chores early. She did not need the

rope today. But when she came in with the milk, she said, "The wind is picking up. It is snowing harder."

Early in the winter, Father had attached a rope to the barn door. He had stretched it to the house and tied it tightly to the porch post.

In a blizzard, you could see nothing. If you were at the barn, you put your arm across the rope and followed it to the house.

Now Joel saw the worry in Mother's eyes as she stirred up the fire. But she spoke cheerfully, "Thank God, we have plenty of wood. Father was smart when he attached the woodshed to the house. We don't need to go outside to get our wood like some people do."

Yes, they could keep warm, but what would they eat?

Mother tipped the meal chest on its side and scooped out a few spoonfuls of meal. With it she made a small dish of mush. Joel ate it for supper, but he did not feel full.

"Drink another cup of milk if you are still hungry," said Mother.

He did so, then went to bed.

All night the wind shrieked around the little house. Fine snow sifted in around the windows.

Tuesday morning before he got up, Joel heard Mother scraping the meal chest and the flour bin. The breakfast mush was nice and hot, but it was as thin as gravy. The last of the meal was gone.

That was yesterday. Now it was Wednesday, and as they got up from their knees, Joel asked, "Mother, will God 'give us this day our daily bread'?"

"Yes, Son," Mother answered, but her voice sounded a little shaky.

"But how can He, unless Father comes home? Do you think he can come in this blizzard?"

"No, Joel. Father could not drive in this storm. We may be hungry for a while, but God will take care of us."

Mother said nothing about her greatest fear—that Father had been caught in the blizzard and frozen to death like other early settlers had.

Joel put Mother's fear into words. "But suppose Father got lost in the blizzard. How would God 'give us this day our daily bread' then?"

"God knows how to handle such things," said Mother, turning away. She did not want her son to see the worry in her face.

"Then Father must be coming soon. I'm going to watch for him."

The boy went to the window. He melted a hole in the frosted glass. He peered out into the storm, but he could see only a solid wall of snow blowing straight across.

Dinnertime came and went. Mother heated some milk for them to drink.

"God didn't give us our daily bread," said Joel as he drank.

"*Bread* means 'food,'" said Mother. "Milk is food. Besides, the day isn't over yet."

Joel went and looked out his peephole. It had always been fun to watch the snow blowing with Father at home and Mother cooking supper. But it was different now with Father gone and no supper to cook.

He peered through the peephole every few minutes, until Mother said, "Joel, you may as well stop looking for Father. He could not get through this storm with the horse and wagon."

Joel took one more look, then cried, "Something is coming! Mother, come look! Doesn't that look like something is coming?"

Before Mother could get her eye to the peephole, they heard a bumping on the porch. Then the door burst open and two snowmen stumbled in, dragging a hand sled.

Their neighbor and his grown son clumped to the stove. Snow fell off them and melted to puddles on the floor. For a while they were too exhausted to talk.

But at last the man said, "We saw your man drive off day before yesterday and knew you must be low in supplies. When this storm lasted so long, we thought we'd better see if you had enough to go on till he got home. We brought you a sack of meal and some potatoes."

"We didn't have a bit of anything left," said Mother,

the tears running down her face. "I didn't know what we were going to do."

"Well, we are glad to help out. And don't you worry about your man. He knows better than to set out when a blizzard is coming. He's safe there in town.

"And he's not worrying about you either. He knows we would see after you till he got back. We came along the fence all the way here and will go home the same way."

The neighbor put the sack of meal on the table along with the bag of potatoes.

"Now we will do your chores, so you don't have to get out in this blizzard. Give us your milk pails."

While the neighbor and his son headed for the barn, Mother quickly peeled some potatoes. She had a pot of steaming potato soup to feed them when they came in with the milk.

Joel sat up to the table and ate some too, because he had had no dinner.

While the men were putting on their boots for the tramp home, Joel said, "God did 'give us this day our daily bread,' after all. I couldn't think how He would do it when the meal chest was empty and the blizzard still blowing. But He had a way all planned. After this we aren't going to worry about anything, because God knows how to handle such things."

—Bertha E. Bush

> *"The word of the Lord endureth for ever."*
> – 1 Peter 1:25

The Rag-Bag Pillow

Bang! Bang! Bang!

Someone hammered on the door of the missionaries' hut—someone who did not sound very friendly.

"Hide the pages, Ann," whispered the missionary, as he jumped up from the table. "I will see if those at the door are friends."

Over 150 years ago Adoniram Judson and his wife Ann went as missionaries to the country of Burma.

Burma lies halfway around the world from America. The people there did not speak English. At that time they did not know much about God and Jesus.

Adoniram and Ann worked hard to learn the Burmese language. How happy they were when they could use Burmese words to tell about Jesus!

But the Burmese people could not talk English to the Judsons. They could not read the English Bible. They could not read the Bible at all because there was no Bible written in the Burmese language.

"We must translate the Bible into the Burmese language," said Adoniram.

Translate means to change the words of one language into the words of another language so that they mean the same thing.

"It will be a long, hard job," said Ann. "We will need many of our Burmese friends to help us know what words to use." So they had begun. Month after month they worked. They translated page after page of the New Testament into Burmese. Their Christian servant helped. Their friends helped. Everyone helped to think of Burmese words that meant the same as the English words in the Bible.

Adoniram wrote down the Bible verses using the Burmese words. Soon they had many pages of Bible verses written in the Burmese language.

One day Adoniram said, "God has been good to us. Before long, our dear Burmese people will be able to read the Bible in their own language."

Ann said, "I just hope nothing happens to the pages before we finish translating. You know some of the people around here do not like Americans. They do not like missionaries."

"I know," said Adoniram. "We must pray that God

will take care of the pages we have translated. I believe He will keep His Word safe."

ॐ   ॐ   ॐ   ॐ   ॐ

Bang! Bang! Bang!

"Adoniram Judson, open this door," rang out a **stern** voice.

"Are the pages out of sight?" he whispered.

"Yes, they are all hidden," said Ann. "You may open the door now."

Adoniram slid back the bar and opened the door. Into the room pushed three men. The Judsons had never seen them before.

"You must come with us," one of them said.

"We are missionaries from America. Why must I go with you? What do you want?"

"We want you!" said the men. "We have been sent to take you to jail!"

"To jail!" cried Ann. "Why? We have done nothing wrong. We want to tell your people about the God who loves them. We want to help you!"

"We have been told to take this man to jail. That is all we know. So get your things and come along."

Adoniram got some clothes and other things. "Take care of the pages," he whispered to Ann as he said good-bye.

The men tied ropes around the missionary and led

him to the dark, dirty jail. Many other men were there. At night they were chained to a long pole so they could not escape.

That night Adoniram could not sleep. No one had told him why he had been put in jail. Maybe it was because he was a Christian missionary. Maybe the men would take Ann away to jail.

Their servant would keep the translated pages safe. But he was a Christian also. What if they put the servant in jail? Then what would become of the Bible for the Burmese people? If the pages were lost, it would take years to translate them again.

"Please, God, take care of Your Word," he prayed.

Ann came to visit him in jail. They talked to each other in English. The other men and the **jailer** could not understand what they were saying.

"Ann, I fear for the pages we have translated," said Adoniram. "What would become of them if something happened to you and to our servant? I wish there were a place here in jail that I could hide them. I would feel better if I had them here with me. Then I would *know* where they are."

"We must keep those pages safe no matter what happens to us," said Ann. "Let me think."

At last she said, "I have a plan. I will send our servant to you with the pages. Be looking for them."

Ann went home. She told the servant her plan. They took the pages from their hiding place. They wrapped them in a kind of paper that would keep them dry.

Then Ann got some old rags. She sewed them around the bundle of pages. She sewed them tightly so none of the pages could be seen or fall out.

"Now," she said to the servant, "take this pillow to Mr. Judson. Tell him he will sleep better tonight if his head is on this pillow."

Ann smiled at the servant and the servant smiled back. Then they prayed that the plan would work.

The servant took the rag pillow to the jail. He said to the jailer, "Here is a pillow for Mr. Judson. His wife made it for him."

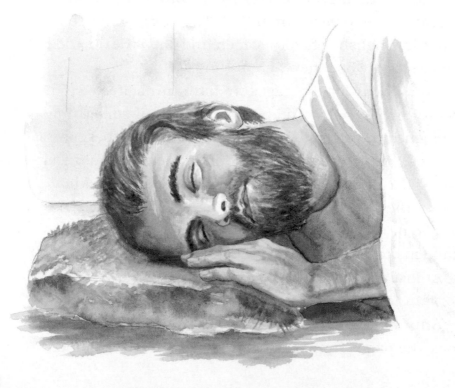

How the jailer laughed! "A pillow! It looks more like a rag bag to me."

He threw the pillow in to Adoniram. "Here is a fine new pillow for you," he said, still laughing. "Just be sure the other men do not steal it."

Adoniram picked up the bundle of rags. He knew what was in that rag-bag pillow. "Thank you," he said. "I will keep it with me all the time. No one will steal it."

Every night after that, Adoniram went to sleep with the rag-bag pillow under his head. Every night he thanked God that the Burmese Bible was safe.

Mr. Judson was kept in jail for almost two years. One day the jailer came and opened the door. "Mr. Judson, you may go free. You may go home now."

"My things," said Adoniram, picking up the pillow. "I must get my things first."

"Never mind your things. They belong to me now. Get on home, if you know what is good for you!"

Adoniram went.

The jailer took all of Mr. Judson's things for his own— all but the rag-bag pillow. "This is nothing but trash," he said. He threw it out on the trash pile.

He did not know that Adoniram's servant saw him throw out the pillow. The servant soon had the pillow safe in the little hut where the missionary lived.

Today when Burmese Christians read the Bible, it is from the translation that was hidden in the rag-bag pillow.

—*Ruth K. Hobbs*

A Strange Wall

Ivan Stravitsky peered out the window of the small house in Russia. The snow had nearly stopped falling, but a strong wind kept the air full of swirling flakes. Every once in a while that afternoon, Ivan had thought he heard a far-off booming sound. Grandmother dozed by the fire with little Lena playing nearby.

Once Ivan had seen Mother glance quickly at Father. But no one had said anything.

Later he had heard the booming again, closer this time. He had gone to the window to see if he could discover what caused the sound. As he watched, there came a **lull** in the wind and a break in the driving snow.

"Oh, look, Father!" he cried. "Come look at the orange glow over there. It must be a fire! I wonder what happened."

The rest of the family rushed to the window. "Why, that has to be the Rimsky's place," Father cried, straining to see through the blowing snow.

"Father!" Ivan cried in alarm, pointing to a different place. "It looks like another fire over there! Whatever can be wrong? Two houses burning!"

Before Father could explain, Lena cried out from the window at the other side of the room. Several faint, glowing lights showed fires burning in the direction of other neighbors' houses.

"What is happening? How could so many catch on fire at the same time?" Ivan asked his father in a **bewildered** voice.

Father sighed. He put his arms around Lena and Ivan and drew them close. "You know there is a war going on, don't you?"

"Yes," said Ivan. "Some people don't like our government and are trying to change it."

"That's right," Father replied. "And the army that is **rebelling** against the government has moved into our area now. The soldiers set fire to houses and barns, hoping it will help them win the war."

As the darkness deepened, the boom of guns grew louder.

"How can they keep fighting with the snow blowing like this?" Mother asked.

"They are so determined to have their way and overthrow the government that nothing will stop them," Father replied.

Every time a lull came in the driving snow, the family caught **glimpses** of the fires flaring up around the countryside. The army seemed to be burning everything in its path.

"What can we do?" Mother Stravitsky asked in a worried voice. "If they force us to leave, we have no place to go. It's so cold. We would freeze."

No one replied to Mother's statement or answered her question.

The family sat silently in the darkness around the table. Ivan shivered. He could imagine the rebel soldiers wading through the deep snow in their direction. At any moment, bullets could crash through the windows.

At last, Father picked up his Bible. "I'll read Psalm 91 before we go to bed," he said. "Let's cover the windows and light the lamp."

Mother and Grandmother hung blankets over the windows. Then Ivan lit the lamp and Father began reading. "'He that dwelleth in the secret place of the most High shall abide under the shadow of the Almighty. I will say of the LORD, He is my **refuge** and my **fortress** . . .'"

I wish we had a secret place to hide in, thought Ivan. *I wish we had a fortress—a real fortress. How can God be a fortress?*

Father read on. "'Thou shalt not be afraid of the terror by night.'" He paused.

"That surely fits," Mother said quietly.

"But how can we *not* be afraid?" Ivan asked, bewildered.

"Because we are God's children, and we know that He will take care of us," Father said.

"But how?" Lena echoed Ivan's thought.

Grandmother smiled. "A song we sang when I was a girl has been going through my mind all evening," she said. "The only line I can remember is 'Build a wall around us.' I think we should ask God to build a wall of protection around us tonight."

Ivan frowned. "But how could He do that? No one could build a wall now with the fires and the shooting so near and with the snow and all."

Grandmother replied calmly, "He will find a way if it is His will, Ivan. God can build a wall without stones or bricks or concrete. Just trust Him."

"That reminds me of something that happened to Elisha when an army came after him," Father said. "Here it is in 2 Kings 6."

Father read how God's army had protected Elisha. Then he said, "You see, Ivan, God surrounded Elisha with horses and chariots of fire."

"That was a kind of a wall, wasn't it?" Mother put in.

"You mean God will put horses and chariots of fire around our house?" Ivan asked wonderingly.

"He certainly could, but it is not likely we would see them any more than Elisha's servant did," Father said. "But if we ask Him, we can be sure He will hear our prayer and protect us according to His will."

The family bowed their heads as Father prayed: "Lord, we need a wall around us to protect us tonight. You know the soldiers are coming through this valley, burning homes as they go. So, Lord, if it is Your will, we ask that You'll put a wall around us so they won't see our house. And we will praise You. In Jesus' name. Amen."

A quiet "Amen" echoed from each person around the table.

At bedtime, Father fixed the fire for the night. Mother put out the lamp and uncovered the windows. The wind still whistled around the house. As they peered into the darkness they could see no fires. However, they still could hear the dull sound of guns—some near, some farther away.

Snug in bed, Ivan could not sleep. The screaming wind and icy snow scratching across the roof made the loft a noisy place. But the noise of the wind did not keep him awake. The guns did. They sounded closer than ever.

Chariots of fire! How he wished the fires around them were God's chariots of fire instead of the burning homes of their neighbors. How he wished for a real fortress—a real refuge they could hide behind.

Then Grandmother's words came back to him. "God can build a wall without stones or bricks or concrete. Just trust Him."

"Just trust Him!" That was easy to say. It wasn't easy to *do* when you knew someone was coming to set fire to your house.

Ivan lay a long time listening to the wind, the snow, and the guns. Finally he whispered, "I want to trust You, God. Please help me. And please make a wall to hide us."

Ivan felt better after he had prayed. However, he was sure he would not sleep, because the last gun had boomed closer than ever. It sounded almost in front of the house.

The next thing Ivan heard was Father's voice downstairs. "Come, everyone! Look at the wall the Lord put around us!" Ivan sat up. It was morning. He had slept after all.

Ivan was down the ladder in no time. He peered out with the rest of the family crowded in the doorway.

At first he saw nothing but a strange, blank whiteness. Then he realized he was looking at a huge snowdrift, higher than the house. God had built a wall of snow all around them. The rebel soldiers had gone on up the valley. They had not seen the little house, safe in its refuge behind its fortress of snow.

–Author Unknown

The Stravitsky family was glad for the snow that fell in the night. The little fellow in this poem likes the snow too.

The Snowbird

When all the ground with snow is white,
    The merry snowbird comes
And hops about with great delight
    To find the scattered crumbs.

How glad he seems to get to eat
    A piece of cake or bread!
He wears no shoes upon his feet
    Nor hat upon his head.

But happiest is he, I know,
    Because no cage with bars
Keeps him from walking on the snow
    And printing it with stars.

–Frank D. Sherman

> *"He went in therefore, and shut the door upon them twain, and prayed unto the LORD."*
>
> – 2 Kings 4:33

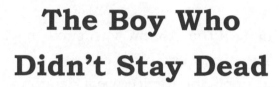

The Boy Who Didn't Stay Dead

18. And when the child was grown, it fell on a day, that he went out to his father to the reapers.
19. And he said unto his father, My head, my head. And he said to a lad, Carry him to his mother.
20. And when he had taken him, and brought him to his mother, he sat on her knees till noon, and then died.
21. And she went up, and laid him on the bed of the man of God, and shut the door upon him, and went out.
27. And when she came to the man of God to the hill, she caught him by the feet: but Gehazi came near to thrust her away. And the man of God said, Let her alone; for her soul is **vexed** within her: and the LORD hath hid it from me, and hath not told me.

28. Then she said, Did I desire a son of my lord? did I not say, Do not deceive me?

29. Then he said to Gehazi, Gird up thy loins, and take my staff in thine hand, and go thy way: if thou meet any man, **salute** him not; and if any salute thee, answer him not again: and lay my staff upon the face of the child.

30. And the mother of the child said, As the Lord liveth, and as thy soul liveth, I will not leave thee. And he arose, and followed her.

31. And Gehazi passed on before them, and laid the staff upon the face of the child; but there was neither voice, nor hearing. Wherefore he went again to meet him, and told him, saying, The child is not awaked.

32. And when Elisha was come into the house, behold, the child was dead, and laid upon his bed.

33. He went in therefore, and shut the door upon them twain, and prayed unto the Lord.

34. And he went up, and lay upon the child, and put his mouth upon his mouth, and his eyes upon his eyes, and his hands upon his hands: and he stretched himself upon the child; and the flesh of the child waxed warm.

35. Then he returned, and walked in the house to and fro; and went up, and stretched himself upon him: and the child sneezed seven times, and the child opened his eyes.

36. And he called Gehazi, and said, Call this Shunammite. So he called her. And when she was come in unto him, he said, Take up thy son.
37. Then she went in, and fell at his feet, and bowed herself to the ground, and took up her son, and went out.

—2 Kings 4:18-21, 27-37

> *"It is even a vapour, that appeareth for a little time, and then vanisheth away."*
>
> – James 4:14

How Can Steam Be Strong?

Years ago, a boy named James Watt lived in faraway Scotland. He and his grandmother lived together in a little cottage.

James was not lonely because there were so many things to see and wonder about. He was always asking his grandmother about something.

One evening as he read

by the fireplace, he heard a slow, sweet singing sound. It came from the teakettle hanging over the fire in the fireplace.

"Grandmother, what is in the teakettle?" he asked.

"Just water," she answered. "Nothing but water."

"But there must be something else. Something is in there singing."

"Oh, that?" Grandmother laughed. "That is the steam. When the water gets close to boiling, it makes that singing sound. You can see some steam coming out of the **spout**."

James watched a while, then went back to his book. Soon he heard a different sound coming from the teakettle. *Clip, clip, clip, clip.*

"Grandmother, the teakettle isn't singing anymore. Now it is going *clip, clip, clip, clip,*" said James. "And see how the steam shoots out of the spout."

"Oh," explained Grandmother, "the water started to boil faster. It is making more steam. The steam can't get out of the spout fast enough, so it lifts the lid and squeezes out. Every time the lid rises up, some steam comes out, then the lid drops back. That clipping sound is the lid dropping down."

"Yes, I see a little puff of steam coming out every time the lid hops up. How strange. Why does the steam have to get out? The water was not trying to get out of the kettle before it got hot."

"I don't know, James," said Grandmother. "Be careful there. You will burn your nose!"

James had laid his book down and gone near the teakettle. He put his face close to watch the lid popping up and down.

Then he took a long-handled fork and held it in the steam puffing from the spout. Next he tipped back the lid.

"Look at the water on the underside of the lid, Grandmother. How did it get there? The water in the kettle is not nearly up to the lid. And now the fork is wet too. I did not stick it in the water."

"Steam is just water, James. For some reason water turns to steam when it gets hot enough. Then when it cools, it turns back to water. The steam against the cooler lid, and your cooler fork, turned back to water. Please do not ask me why or how, for I do not know.

"And now I must take the kettle off the fire or the water will all boil away."

Grandmother swung the teakettle from over the fire and soon it stopped singing.

James went back to his book, but he was not thinking of the words printed there.

Soon he said, "Grandmother, when the steam comes out of the kettle it disappears into the air and goes to nothing. But in the kettle it is strong enough to lift the lid. Why is it strong in the kettle, but not outside the kettle?"

"James, James," said Grandmother. "I do not know. I am sorry I cannot tell you."

"That is all right, Grandmother," replied James.

He really did not expect Grandmother to know the answers to such questions. Much of the time he was just thinking out loud anyway.

"It seems to me if the steam from the teakettle is strong enough to make the lid move, it could move other things. We could **accomplish** a lot if we could make steam work for us somehow. Someday I mean to find out. Someday I will see how strong steam is."

When James Watt grew to be a man, he began to work with steam and to find ways to use it.

Other men were also working with steam. One had invented a steam engine; but it did not work very well, so it did not accomplish much.

James began to improve the steam engine that was already invented. Little by little he improved it until it worked much better. His improvements made it possible to accomplish much more with the steam engine. In fact, most people today believe that James Watt invented the steam engine in the first place.

James did invent quite a few things that had nothing to do with steam. He even invented a word—*horse-power*—which we use today.

And the word *watt,* which we use to tell how much light a bulb makes, was chosen in honor of James Watt.

—Ruth K. Hobbs

James Watt never heard a train whistle when he was a boy. Do you know why?

Trains at Night

I like the whistle of trains at night,
The fast trains thundering by so proud!
They rush and rumble across the world;
They ring wild bells and they toot so loud!

But I love better the slower trains.
They take their time through the world instead.
And whistle softly and stop to tuck
Each sleepy, blinking town in bed!

—Frances M. Frost

I Cannot

A shepherd boy named Herman and his dog were watching his master's sheep in a little valley in Germany. No fences surrounded the pastures. Herman's job was to keep track of the sheep as they **grazed** among the bushes. At night he would lead them back to his master's barn.

Nearby grew a forest that was well known as a good place to hunt deer and other game.

Around noon, a lone hunter came out of the forest. When he saw Herman, he asked, "How far is it to the nearest village where I can buy something to eat and drink?"

"Nearly six miles, sir," replied Herman. "But the path from here is only a sheep track most of the way. You could easily get lost unless you have gone that way before."

The hunter glanced at the crooked track winding away through the bushes. "My lad, I have lost my hunting companions. I am tired and hungry and thirsty. I will pay you well if you will guide me to the village."

"I am very sorry, sir," said Herman. "I would gladly lead you there, but I cannot leave my master's sheep. By the time I would return, who knows what would have happened to them? Wolves or even robbers could get them. At the very least, they would stray away where I could not find them."

"What of that?" asked the hunter. "The sheep do not belong to you. The loss of one or more would not mean much to your master. I dare say he is rich enough. At any rate, I would pay you more than he probably pays you in a whole year."

"I cannot go. It is my **duty** to take care of my master's sheep and to see that no harm comes to them," said Herman firmly. "I cannot leave them alone no matter how much you might pay me."

"Well, then, I will give you money to go and buy what I need and hire a guide for me. I will keep an eye on your sheep. No harm will come to them. It will not take you long to go and come, since you know the path well."

Again the boy shook his head. "I am very sorry. I would gladly guide you to the village. But my time is not my own. My master pays me for it. I cannot hire myself out to you. Neither do I have the right to hire you to care for the sheep while I go to the village. My master trusts *me* with his sheep. I must care for them myself. I cannot trust them to a stranger."

"What do you mean? Why can you not trust me? Do I look like a person who would break his word?"

"No, sir," said Herman. "You look honest enough. Yet you want me to break my word to my master. How do I know you would not break your word to me?

"You have said it would not matter if some of the sheep were lost. Suppose your companions came while I was gone? Would you stay with the sheep until I returned?"

The hunter remained silent. Then after a moment he said, "You are a good, **faithful** boy. Show me the path and I will try to find my way to the village alone."

Herman then offered his lunch to the man. He had nothing but dark bread and cheese made from goat's milk, but the man ate hungrily.

Before he had finished, his hunting companions burst from the forest, very glad to find their friend.

Then to his great astonishment, Herman learned that he had been talking with the ruler of the whole country, the Grand Duke himself.

The Duke was so pleased with Herman's courage and faithfulness that sometime later he sent for the boy. "My lad, I would like to do something for you. What do you most need?"

"Sir," said Herman, "my parents are very poor. I must

work all the time so that we have enough to eat. If only I could go to school, I would be so happy."

"You shall indeed go to school," said the Duke, much pleased with Herman's reply. "I will pay for your schooling and see that your parents are well cared for until you can work for them again. I wish all the people in our country knew that honesty and faithfulness are more important than money."

–adapted

Billfold Mystery

"Jem, I have dropped my billfold somewhere out here in the field. Have you seen it?" asked Mr. Evans of the boy who was hoeing potatoes for him.

"No, sir, I have not," replied Jem, stopping his work. "What color was it? Would you like Barker and me to help look for it?"

"Yes, I wish you would, though I don't suppose your dog will be of much help. The billfold is dark brown. You go on that side of the field along the road toward the gate. I will look on this side."

"All right," said Jem cheerfully. He dropped his hoe in the **furrow**. Then whistling to his dog, he started along the edge of the field.

Barker sniffed along, too, but soon began barking at a groundhog hole in a rock pile. Then he barked at Freddie Blake walking by with a fishing pole. Next, he

216

barked at a crow on a fence post and at Mr. Harlow coming from town in his wagon.

Finally, a rabbit popped out of the weeds and Barker took off after it toward the woods, barking all the way.

"You really aren't much help," said Jem with a laugh, as he watched the dog disappear. Then he moved slowly on, scanning the ground carefully for a dark brown billfold.

When he reached the gate, he found Mr. Evans there already with the billfold in his hand.

"Oh, you have found it. I am glad of that," said Jem, looking pleased.

"Yes, I have found it. I guess you knew where it was all the time since I found it here on the grass beside your lunch box. You did a good job of pretending you knew nothing about it."

Jem's mouth dropped open in astonishment. "But, sir, I don't know anything about it. Truly I don't. I do not know how it got there beside my lunch box. I did not see it when I put my box here after I ate dinner."

"Oh, you look **innocent** enough," snapped the farmer, "but thieves are good at looking innocent."

Hot, angry words rushed to Jem's lips, but just then Barker's cool nose pushed into his hand. The dog whined as if he knew something was wrong.

Jem leaned over and patted Barker while he blinked back the angry tears that started in his eyes.

Then he straightened up and said quietly, "If I meant to steal your billfold, do you think I would have put it in plain sight there on the grass?"

Mr. Evans blinked a few times at these words. He could not answer Jem's question. It made him angry to think he might have been wrong.

"Well then, young man," he **sputtered**, "explain how it came to be lying beside your lunch box."

"I don't know, sir," admitted Jem, who by this time had gotten over his anger. "But I know I did not steal it or put it there."

"I cannot believe that because I have the proof right here," said the farmer. "I don't want a thief and a liar working for me, so you may quit as soon as you like.

"I will mail what I owe you to your parents, and I will let them know why I **fired** you. You would not likely tell them the truth."

Jem was so astonished and hurt by this sudden turn of events that he could not say a word. He picked up the lunch box and went directly home, followed by Barker.

He told the whole story to his mother and closed by saying, "You believe me, don't you, Mother?"

"Yes, Jem," she replied. "I am sure you did not take Mr. Evans' billfold. I have no idea how the billfold got there beside your lunch box. We may never know that. But Jesus knows who put it there."

This comforted Jem a great deal. When his father came home and heard the story, he said, "Jem, Jesus was **accused** of doing wrong too. Now you know a little about how He must have felt. But I want you to remember one thing that Jesus never did. When lies were told about Him, He never told others how He had been treated. He had done nothing wrong, so He was satisfied to have pleased His heavenly Father."

"I will try to be that way too," promised Jem, "though I feel like telling everyone how Mr. Evans treated me."

Mr. Evans did send Jem's money and wrote the letter as he had promised. Jem did not find out what the farmer had written for, after taking out the money, Father read the letter. Then he smiled at Jem and dropped it into the stove.

But that did not end the matter, for Mr. Evans told the story all around. Some believed the farmer. Some believed Jem to be innocent. "It can't be. There must be some mistake, for Jem always has been an honest boy," they said.

Jem knew his friends had heard Mr. Evans' story. They knew the farmer told others he had stolen the billfold. How he longed to tell them his side of the story. Many times he had to remind himself that Jesus was with him and knew exactly how he felt.

After a number of days, Mr. Harlow stopped by and asked to talk with Jem.

"I need a boy to work for me. Would you be able to come?"

"I will have to ask my parents," said Jem. "But are you sure you want me? Haven't you heard about Mr. Evans' billfold?"

"Yes," said Mr. Harlow. "I know more about it than you do. I was going to town in my wagon that day. I saw your dog with the billfold in his mouth trotting along a furrow toward your lunch box. When I saw you in the field, I supposed the billfold belonged to you.

"Yesterday I heard that Mr. Evans has accused you of stealing his billfold. I have asked quite a few people about it, but everyone says you will not talk. Now that's the kind of boy I like. That is why I want you to work for me."

So Mr. Harlow solved the mystery. Moreover, Mr. Harlow told Mr. Evans and everyone else how it all happened.

Of course that made Jem happy, but he felt happier yet when he remembered that he had done just as Jesus had when people falsely accused Him.

—adapted

"A man shall be commended according to his wisdom."

– Proverbs 12:8

Think Fast

Once there was a good old man who lived with his grandson on a mountain in far-off Japan. The mountain ran down to the sea, where a tiny village lay between it and the water.

There was no land for crops around the village. For that reason the people had cut terraces on the mountainside. A terrace is a narrow strip of level land. Many of these terraces were cut, one above the other, on the side of the mountain. On each terrace the village people had planted rice.

Grandfather and Kenzo could look down on the people in the village. They could look far out over the blue sea to where it met the blue sky.

Kenzo and his grandfather knew and loved the people of the village. The men and women would climb the steep paths to the rice terraces to tend their precious

222

crop of rice. Kenzo knew that food for the whole village grew on the terraces. Rice was the main food of the people who lived there.

Now the rice stalks drooped dry and heavy with the rice grains. Soon the villagers could harvest the crop.

One day the grandfather stood alone before his house. He gazed down at the village and out over the sea. Suddenly he saw something **extremely** strange out where the sea and the sky met. There, something like a great cloud **billowed** into the air. It seemed as if the sea were climbing into the sky. The old man shaded his eyes with his hand and looked again. Then he turned and ran to the house.

"Kenzo, Kenzo!" he cried. "Bring a stick from the fire and come to the rice fields. Run!"

Kenzo could not understand what his grandfather wanted with fire, but he did as he was told. He ran into the house and pulled a burning stick from the fire.

His grandfather had reached the nearest rice terrace. He was holding a burning stick to the dry rice stalks.

"Grandfather, Grandfather!" screamed the boy. "What are you doing?"

"Quick, set the rice afire!" shouted Grandfather, waving his arm toward another terrace.

Kenzo thought his grandfather had lost his mind.

He began to cry, but did as he was told. He held his burning stick against the rice. A sharp red and yellow flame ran up the stems.

In a moment fire swept across the field. Clouds of thick black smoke billowed upward.

Soon the people in the village below saw the burning rice fields. How they screamed and ran. Men and young people raced for the rice fields. Women grabbed their babies and with their children scrambled up the steep mountain paths. They ran as fast as they could, hoping to save the rice. Not one stayed in the village.

But they came too late. When they arrived, the terraces flamed beyond control.

"Who did this thing? What started it? How did it happen?" shouted the people **furiously**.

"I set the fire," said Grandfather quietly.

"Grandfather made me help," said Kenzo through his tears.

Everyone gathered around the old man screaming, "Why, why?"

The old man turned and pointed toward the sea. "Look," he said.

They all turned and looked. And there, instead of the quiet blue sea, a high wall of water came rolling toward the land. No one could scream, so terrible was the sight.

The wall of water raced in and roared over the village. It broke with a great thunder on the mountainside.

Another wave followed that, and still one more came. Then the water drained back into the sea.

The people on the mountain stood **speechless**, looking down to where their village had stood. Not a house, not a shop, not a stick remained of their homes.

But all the people were safe. And when they realized what the old man had done, they gathered around him with tears and cries of thanksgiving. By burning some of their rice fields, he had saved everyone from the **tidal wave**.

–Lafcadia Hearn

> *"I was eyes to the blind."*
> – Job 29:15

Finger Reading

In the year 1809, a baby boy was born into the Braille family in the country of France. The parents named the new baby Louis.

Louis had two sisters and a brother. The oldest was Catherine, who was fifteen. She helped with the housework. Next came Simon, who was thirteen. He was learning to be a harness maker like his father. Then came Marie, who was eleven and a big help on the farm.

When Louis was a baby, Marie sang songs to him. When he was two years old, Catherine began to tell him stories she had read. When he was three, Simon and his father began to take him into the harness shop.

Louis liked to play with bits of leather in the harness shop. He like to watch his father and Simon work. One day he picked up an **awl** and tried to punch it through a scrap of leather. The awl did not go through. Louis held the leather up before his eyes and shoved the awl against it with all his strength. The awl slipped and **punctured** his eye.

His parents took Louis to many doctors. They did everything they knew to do, but they could not save the little boy's eye.

Each day Louis saw less and less out of the punctured eye. Finally he could see nothing at all from that eye.

Before long the sight in the other eye began to grow dim. Then one day Louis realized he could not see anything at all. He would be blind the rest of his life. He would have to learn to live in darkness.

And learn he did. He was a happy child and did not feel sorry for himself. At home he memorized how many steps it took to reach the table from the door of the dining room. He learned the number of steps to the big chair by the window.

The family always kept the furniture in the same place so that Louis would know where he could walk. Before long, he could go about the house without bumping into anything.

Since Louis couldn't use his eyes, he learned to use his ears, his fingers, and his nose to find out about things. He discovered that every person's voice sounded different from every other voice. He learned that every person's footsteps played a different tune. Slow, even footsteps meant Papa was coming. Fast, light footsteps told him Marie went by.

Louis learned much about the outside world too. He took long walks with Marie. He listened to the different birdcalls. He smelled and felt the flowers.

At first Marie described things to Louis. Then he began to tell her what he learned by listening.

"There is a nest of baby birds in that tall tree, Marie," he said one day, pointing up to a tree.

"Why, Louis," she cried, "I can't see any nest. I don't hear anything. How do you even know there is a tree there?"

Louis laughed and said, "I hear little birds cheeping high up. So I know there must be a nest of baby birds in a tall tree, even though I can't see a tree or a nest or any baby birds."

Louis enjoyed school and listened closely to all the interesting things his teacher said. He remembered them and could repeat everything in the lesson, if anyone asked him.

Of course, Louis had not been able to learn the alphabet because he could not see. Finally his teacher thought of a good plan for teaching it to him. He made the letters out of twigs so Louis could feel the shapes of the ABCs. Then he put letters together and taught Louis how they made words.

"Now I can read!" Louis cried happily. "I want to read

stories in books. There are books I can read, aren't there?"

"Yes, there are books you can read with your fingers," the teacher said. "But we don't have any in our school. They are at a school for the blind in Paris. Perhaps someday you will be able to go to the school in that city."

When he turned ten years old, Louis' parents did send him to that school for the blind in Paris, France. There his teachers showed him a book he could read.

The enormous book was kept on a stand. The words were written in large raised letters. Louis felt the shapes of the letters with the tips of his fingers. Slowly he spelled out the words. At last he could read a book. He was delighted.

Louis read all of that book. He read several others. Then he asked for more.

"We're sorry. Those are all the books we have for the blind," he was told. "Those books cost so much that only a few of them have ever been made."

Louis understood that it would take many of those enormous books of raised letters to hold the stories in one small school reader. That is why they cost so much. How he wished the books were not so **expensive** so that more could be made.

One day the school invited an army captain to visit the school. He explained a new kind of writing to the teachers and the blind pupils. He called it night-writing.

The captain used dots and dashes punched in cardboard for the night-writing. The dots and dashes stood for letters. He told them that even in the dark, soldiers could read messages with their fingertips. He showed how blind people could also read raised dots and dashes, although they were not real words.

At first Louis was delighted. Raised dots and dashes seemed like an answer to the problem of reading without eyes.

But after a while he found that many things about dots and dashes made them much too hard to read. He thought of several ways that night-writing could be made easier.

The teachers asked the captain to come back and talk with Louis, but he would not listen to any changes Louis suggested. Then Louis decided to find a new way by himself. He would use the idea of the raised dots.

Louis spent long hours **experimenting**. He wanted to invent a way of writing that could be used to write many books. He wanted to find a way that would take less space than raised letters. He wanted to discover a way of writing that would be fast and easy to read with the fingers.

And Louis did invent a way of writing and reading for blind people. He did not use raised letters. He used a group of six raised dots—two columns of three dots. Each letter of the alphabet was one or more dots at a certain place in the group. After his fingers memorized the dots that stood for each letter of the alphabet, it did not take long to learn to read words with the tips of his fingers.

Today blind people read storybooks, schoolbooks, and the Bible by running their fingers over raised dots. This kind of reading is called *braille*. Can you guess why?

–Bernice Frankel

Fanny Crosby was six weeks old when she lost her sight. In her lifetime, she wrote thousands of hymns. If you look in your songbook at church or school, you will probably find hymns written by Fanny. She wrote this poem when she was eight years old.

Blind but Happy

O what a happy soul am I!
   Although I cannot see,
I am resolved that in this world
   Contented I will be;
How many blessings I enjoy
   That other people don't!
To weep and sigh because I'm blind
   I cannot, and I won't.

–Fanny Crosby

The two people in this poem couldn't run and play,
although neither of them was blind. Yet they found a way to
play a game that usually takes a lot of running.

One, Two, Three

It was an old, old, old, old lady,
   And a boy who was half-past three;
And the way they played together
   Was beautiful to see.

She couldn't go running and jumping,
   And the boy, no more could he;
For he was a thin little fellow,
   With a thin little twisted knee.

They sat in the yellow sunlight,
   Out under the maple tree;
And the game that they played
     I'll tell you,
   Just as it was told to me.

It was Hide-and-Go-Seek they were
          playing,
   Though you'd never have known it to be—
With an old, old, old, old lady,
   And a boy with a twisted knee.

The boy would bend his face down
   On his one little sound right knee,
And he'd guess where she was hiding,
   In guesses One, Two, Three!

"You are in the china closet!"
   He would cry, and laugh with glee—
It wasn't the china closet;
   But he still had Two and Three.

"You are up in Papa's big bedroom
   In the chest with the queer old key!"
And she said, "You are warm and
          warmer;
   But you're not quite right," said she.

"It can't be the little cupboard
   Where Mama's things used to be—
So it must be the closet, Gran'ma!"
   And he found her with his Three.

Then she covered her face with her
        fingers,
  That were wrinkled and white and wee,
And she guessed where the boy was
        hiding,
  With a One and a Two and a Three.

And they never had stirred from their places,
  Right under the maple tree—
This old, old, old, old lady,
  And the boy with a lame little knee—
This dear, dear, dear, old lady,
And the boy who was half-past three.

                    –H. C. Bunner

How would you answer the questions this poem asks?

How Do You Know It's Spring?

How do you know it's Spring?
And how do you know it's Fall?
Suppose your eyes were always shut
And you couldn't see at all.
Could you smell and hear the Spring?
And could you feel the Fall?

–Margaret W. Brown

> *"Better is the end of a thing than the beginning thereof."*
>
> – Ecclesiastes 7:8

How Tom Earned
Miss Stubbs

Tom had come to spend a month on his grand-father's farm. The sounds that met his ears that first morning were very different from those he usually heard in the city.

There he always heard cars going by the house. Here the roosters woke him. A crow called from the edge of the woods. Somewhere near the barn a cow was mooing at the top of her voice. From the **orchard** he heard another noise which he could not quite make out.

He got up and went to the window. There on the other side of the orchard wall he saw a young calf. It was tied to a stake driven into the ground. Every time the cow mooed, the calf **bawled** an answer.

Tom dressed and hurried downstairs and out to the

238

barn to watch his grandfather feed the farm animals.

"Why does the cow keep making such a noise?" asked Tom.

"I've just taken her calf away, Tom. We need its mother's milk for ourselves. Now the calf must learn how to drink milk out of a pail," his grandfather replied.

"May I teach it?" asked the lad. "I'll take it some milk. I can do it."

Tom's two cousins, George and Frank, who were busy milking, laughed. They knew Tom was asking for a hard job.

Grandfather smiled. "Teaching a calf to drink from a pail is not easy or pleasant, Tom. It takes a great deal of patience. You can't just carry a pail of milk to the calf and expect it to drink."

"I'd like to try, Grandfather," said Tom. "Please let me."

"Well," said Grandfather, "I'll tell you what I will do. I will give that calf to you for your own if you can teach her to drink from a pail. It will take a lot of work. If a boy your size can do that, you will have earned the calf. But you must not beat her or lose your temper, no matter what she does. Remember she is not being stubborn. She is just a baby."

Tom rushed into the house and asked his grand-mother to tell him what to do. She explained how to go about it and gave him a pail with some milk in it. He carried it out to where the calf stood.

His grandmother had told him not to be afraid, for a calf will not bite, and it had no horns.

Tom reached for the calf and held the pail under its nose. Then he dipped his finger into the milk and placed it in the calf's mouth as Grandmother had **instructed**. He was half afraid the calf would bite, but she didn't.

For a moment she did nothing but hold Tom's finger. She stood with her feet spread wide apart. Her tail stuck out—straight out. Suddenly, with a glad leap, she thrust her head down into the pail.

Her head came out white to the eyes with milk. Then looking into Tom's face she gave a big "Whoosh!" Milk **spattered** him from head to foot.

He set the pail down and wiped the milk out of his eyes. Hearing a low laugh, he looked around and saw that Grandfather, George, and Frank stood watching him.

He laughed too, then turned back to the calf. This time he did not hold the pail up to the calf. He set it on the ground. Then he dipped his fingers into the milk and held them toward the calf.

Suddenly up went her hind legs and down went her head. One bound and she had knocked Tom flat on his back with the milk pail on top of him.

When Tom went back to the house, his grandmother asked, "Well, Tom, are you going to give up?"

"No, ma'am," said Tom. "I came after some more milk."

❧   ❧   ❧   ❧   ❧

It took a long time for Tom to earn that calf. It cost much hard work too.

One day the calf stepped into the pail. All the milk spattered over Tom's feet and legs.

Sometimes the calf slapped him across the face with her tail. At other times she would run around him two or three times until the rope bound both of them to the stake. Then Tom found it hard to control his temper.

Once she tried to swallow his hand, and he lost count of the times she knocked him down when she didn't get the milk as fast as she wanted it. At such times Tom thought his grandfather must be wrong. The calf seemed plain stubborn to him. That's when he named her Miss Stubbs.

"Grandfather, are you sure this calf is not stubborn?" he asked one day after Miss Stubbs had knocked the pail over three times in a row. "She seems determined not to drink out of that pail!"

"Are you ready to give up?" asked Grandfather.

"Oh, no," cried Tom. "I like Miss Stubbs even if she is stubborn. I guess I am not such a good teacher after all. She doesn't seem to be learning anything."

"Just stick with it, Tom," said Grandfather. "She is learning more than you think."

So Tom stuck with it.

In between feedings Tom would pet Miss Stubbs and talk to her. He liked to go to the orchard just to be with her. Now she bawled for him instead of for her mother, who seemed to have forgotten all about her. Tom was more determined than ever to win Miss Stubbs for his own.

Then one day Miss Stubbs began to drink as soon as Tom put the pail under her nose. He had no more trouble after that.

When Tom told them that the calf had learned to drink from the pail at last, Grandfather, Grandmother, George, and Frank all came to watch.

After he had fed the calf, Grandfather said, "Well, my boy, you have had quite a time. You have worked hard and didn't lose your temper. I say you have earned your calf. Miss Stubbs belongs to you."

—Edward W. Frentz

Did Tom follow the advice that this poem gives?

Try, Try Again

'Tis a lesson you should heed—
   Try, try again;
If at first you don't succeed,
   Try, try again;
Then your courage should appear,
For, if you will persevere,
You will conquer, never fear;
   Try, try again.

— T. H. Palmer

Do you think Tom produced any of what this poem talks about as he worked with Miss Stubbs?

Produce Your Own

If the string is in a knot
  Patience will untie it.
Patience can do many things,
  Did you ever try it?

If 'twas sold in any shop,
  I should like to buy it.
But we all must find our own;
  Others can't supply it.

–Anna M. Pratt

> *"The earth is full of the goodness of the Lord."*
>
> – Psalm 33:5

Luck or Blessing?

Far across the ocean in the country of Holland, a boy's quick ears caught a strange sound. Spring had arrived, and far above the **thatched** roof of the cottage, Hans heard a strange, faint, clapping noise.

"Do you hear what I hear, Gretel?" he called to his little sister, who ran quickly to his side.

As Gretel turned her round blue eyes up toward the sky, her two yellow pigtails hung far down her back. Mother came to the door of the cottage to listen too.

"Yes, I hear them," cried Gretel. "Surely that sound is the clapping of stork bills. The storks are coming back to build their nests. Oh, now I see them, Hans! They are coming this way. Do you think any of them will build a nest on your wagon wheel?"

Hans watched the flock of huge white storks against the blue Holland sky. "Oh, I hope they build on my wagon wheel. I got it up on the roof just in time," he said.

"Storks will bring us good luck if they build on our roof," said Gretel. "That's what everyone says."

"How could birds make good things happen to people?" asked Hans.

"Good things come from the good God, not from storks," said Mother with a smile. "But it would be nice to have storks on our roof. They would eat the snakes and lizards and insects in the garden."

"Well, that would be a kind of good luck," said Gretel.

"That is a **blessing**, not luck," said Mother.

As the birds came nearer and nearer, the children could see their wide wings and hear the clapping of their bills more plainly.

Storks have no voices, but they make up for this by the clattering and clap-clapping of their heavy bills. This clapping is the first sound people hear when the storks return to the villages every spring.

Now two great white birds dropped toward the housetops, flying in a circle above the thatched cottages.

Hans said, "They are deciding which roof they will build on. I hope they choose my wagon wheel."

Lower and lower circled the big birds. At last one of the storks dropped to the roof of the house. He stood there on one long red leg, eyeing the wagon wheel. His feathers shone like fresh snow.

Then he rose in the air and flew away clattering his bill.

"He saw my wheel. He knows we want him. He will tell his mate and come back," cried Hans.

The next morning the children ran to look at the roof. There some sticks lay on the wagon wheel. A pair of storks had indeed begun to **construct** their nest.

The father stork danced, flapped his wings, and clattered his bill. How funny to see him hopping and skipping about! Every day the pair brought more and more sticks. Soon they had a big nest on the wagon wheel.

Hans and Gretel took care never to frighten the birds, and they became very tame. They stalked around the garden and the fields in search of food.

After a while the mother stork began to stay on the nest all the time. Then the children knew she had laid some eggs.

One morning Gretel saw a baby stork sticking its long bill over the edge of the nest. One egg had hatched!

She ran to tell Mother and Hans the great news. "The baby storks are hatching. And one of them is already out of the shell," she cried.

That day the children hurried home from school to watch the father stork and his mate. The two big birds stayed busy feeding their babies.

"Now we will have lots of good luck," said Gretel. "Look at all the storks we have on our roof."

"You mean God has blessed us with more insect and lizard eaters," said Hans.

"Everybody believes storks bring good luck," Gretel said.

"I don't. Father and Mother don't. Someday you will see that we are right," replied her brother.

"Maybe you will find out everybody else is right," replied Gretel.

A few days later, Hans came home from school early. As he came near the cottage, he saw the storks flapping around the housetop in a strange way. Then he saw a thin line of dark smoke rising from the roof.

Hans ran as fast as he could for he knew his mother had planned to be gone that afternoon. He saw that a corner of the thatched roof was on fire. "Our house and the baby storks will burn if I don't put out the fire," he whispered wildly to himself.

Quickly Hans brought the ladder and set it against the roof. Then he grabbed a pail, filled it with water, and climbed to the roof.

Swish. He dashed the water on the burning thatch. The fire hissed and went out, but sprang up at another place nearby.

Again and again Hans ran down the ladder for another pail of water. His arms ached and the smoke burned his eyes and throat, but he could not stop for that.

Little by little, he soaked the thatched roof and the fire in the kitchen below. At last it was out. Nothing but a **charred** hole remained.

With a great clapping of bills, the storks dropped down to the roof and stood over their babies. Hans dropped the pail and sank to the ground, too tired to move.

In another minute, his mother and some neighbors came running up. They had seen the smoke. Then Gretel came from school. They looked at the charred roof with wide, scared eyes.

"Hans, you have saved our house. You are a brave, brave boy," cried his mother with tears in her eyes.

"I am glad the baby storks did not get burned," exclaimed Gretel.

"I am so glad I came in time to save them," said Hans. "I did only what had to be done."

Then Mother asked, "Gretel, is this the good luck our storks brought us?"

"Well, they didn't start the fire," said the little girl.

"They surely didn't help put it out either," said Hans. "All they did was fly around and clap their bills. It was only the good God in Heaven who helped me save the house. Gretel, you are big enough and smart enough to stop talking about luck."

The little girl stood still. She looked at the charred hole in the roof. She looked at the big white storks clapping their bills softly to their babies. "Yes, you are right," she said. "I'm glad God blessed us by helping you save our house."

−Eleanor Hammond

The Secret

We have a secret, just we three,
The robin and I and the sweet cherry tree;
The bird told the tree and the tree told me,
And nobody knows it but just we three.

Of course the robin knows it best
Because she built the—I shan't tell the rest—
And laid the four little somethings in it—
I'm afraid I shall tell it any minute!

But if the tree and the robin don't peep,
I'll try my best the secret to keep,
But I know when the baby birds
   fly about—
Then the secret
   will all be out!

—Author Unknown

> *"Boast not thyself of tomorrow."*
> – Proverbs 27:1

Little Fox, Man of the Family

Little Fox hurried down the snowy hillside with his dog ahead of him. He tried to run but could not, for he carried a wild turkey in one hand and his bow and arrows in the other.

Little Fox gave an owl call to tell his mother of his approach. When he reached the round bark wigwam, he told his dog to stay outside. Then he pushed aside the skin that covered the doorway and crept in.

His mother, Singing Water, was at home alone. His father, Big Fox, and all the men of the Indian village had gone away on a long hunt. Little Fox was the man of the family until his father returned.

Being the man of the family was hard work. He had helped his mother as much as he could by **snaring** birds and small animals for them to eat. He had never shot a turkey before. It would be a good change from the rabbit and squirrel he had gotten before.

The turkey made Singing Water happy. She said, "My son, someday you will be a great hunter like your father. I wish he would come home. The hunters have been gone more than a moon already. I hope nothing has happened to them.

"But come, I cooked a stew for your supper. After you have brought in water and firewood for the night, we will eat. Then I will show you what I have made for you today."

Little Fox put away his bow and arrows in a hurry. Then he brought in plenty of wood and water.

Singing Water dipped stew from the cooking jar into a wooden bowl. She brought the corncakes she had baked on the stones of the fire. The good hot food disappeared fast.

"Now, what did you make me, Mother? Is it **moccasins**?" Little Fox looked down at his old moccasins with holes in the toes.

"No, not moccasins. I will make you a new pair soon. I have made you this deerskin bag to hang around your waist. Now you can carry the knife your father made for you before he left."

"I feel like a man when I carry my own knife," said Little Fox. "I will skin all the rabbits after this."

His mother smiled. "My son, be careful what you say. Skinning a rabbit is harder than you think. It is better to just *do* something than to brag about what you think you are *going* to do."

Little Fox lay quietly on a mat by the fire. His legs, arms, and shoulders ached. He thought about his mother's words. She was right. Every day since the hunters had left, he had told Singing Water he would bring home a turkey. Many an arrow disappeared forever in the forest while a turkey sped unhurt through the trees. Until today he had been able to kill or snare only small game.

Now he wished he had not bragged that he would shoot a turkey. It would have been better to surprise Singing Water by walking into the wigwam with the turkey. That's the way his father did. His father did not brag about what he could do. He just did it.

Then Little Fox's mind turned to his father. He said, "I wonder where the hunters went and why they don't come home. I will be glad when I am old enough to go

with them. I want to hunt deer and bear and sleep out under the stars. That would be easier than trying to be the man of the family."

But his mother said, "The hunters have a hard life. I would rather work at home and sit by our fire in the wintertime."

Outside it grew colder. Singing Water had partly closed the smoke hole to make the wigwam warmer. Now and then the wind stirred the grass mats that hung on the walls to keep out the cold.

Also around the walls hung baskets. Singing Water had made these to hold different things. She stored nuts in one and dried corn in another. One basket held Little Fox's own treasures. He had put the tail feathers of the turkey in it. He would use them the next time he made arrows.

The warm fire made Little Fox sleepy. Finally he crawled onto his sleeping mat. It was not a soft bed, but it was warm with beaver skins. Soon he was asleep.

Many cold days passed. Little Fox made sure his mother had plenty of wood. He checked his snares every day for rabbits and birds. He brought down squirrels with his bow and arrows. But he never got another turkey. Now his new deerskin bag always hung around his waist. But he wished he had not bragged about skinning every rabbit he caught. It took him so long he wondered how his mother could do it so fast and clean.

Then came some days as warm as spring. Big Fox

and the other hunters had been gone nearly two moons. Singing Water was afraid something had happened to them. She went to the wise old men of the village to ask what they thought.

The older men talked about what should be done. Should they send out young men to find the hunters? They had never been away so long before without sending back a runner. What could have happened?

They decided to wait one more week and then send out a searching party.

Every day Little Fox climbed the highest tree on the highest hill and looked far up the broad river where it disappeared into the forest. That was the way the hunters had gone. He hoped to be the first to see them coming. How he longed for his father to return.

One day he came running into the village. "They are coming, they are coming! I saw the long boats far up the river," he shouted.

At once, all the people ran out of the wigwams.

Some of the young Indians pushed a boat into the river and began paddling off to meet them. Perhaps the hunters would be glad for another boat to help carry the game they had gotten.

Singing Water and the other women hurried to make big fires. How they would feast that night!

Little Fox could hardly wait for his father to arrive. At last the boats pulled ashore.

The hunters' boats were full of skins. There were beaver, deer, bear, and fox skins—piles and piles of them. There would be plenty of skins to make new clothes and moccasins for all.

The hunters also brought fresh deer meat and piles and piles of meat that they had dried. There would be plenty of food for everyone during the cold moons. It was the greatest hunt the village people could remember.

"Why were you gone so long, my father?" asked Little Fox. "We worried about you."

Big Fox smiled. "We found so much game that we just could not stop hunting and drying the meat. We knew if the winter were long and hard, we would need everything we could bring."

Now the women began cooking the fresh meat on poles over the fires.

That night all the men, women, children, and dogs in the village ate their fill.

After the feast, everyone sat around the big fires while the men told stories of what they had seen and done on the hunt.

But for Little Fox the best time of all came when he and Big Fox and Singing Water gathered around their own fire in their own snug wigwam. He was glad he was no longer the man of the family.

−Katharine Keeler

> *"Love ye therefore the stranger."*
>
> – Deuteronomy 10:19

The Missing Quilt

Part 1

Carol led Maria Teresa into the Sunday school room. "Sister Ruby, this is my new friend, Maria Teresa Pinzarro. Her family came across the ocean from Italy not very long ago. They live on our street."

"From Italy? How nice," said Sister Ruby. "Our Bible story today is about the Apostle Paul who went to Italy. He was in a shipwreck."

"We no have shipwreck," said Maria Teresa with a smile that showed white teeth. "We come from Eetaly in airplane."

"When we have our lesson, we would like for you to show us on the map where your home was in Italy.

"But now, Carol will show you around our room until

the other children come."

Carol showed the little Italian girl the ribbons where they pasted the memory verses. She showed the pictures where they put a sticker each time they came to Sunday school.

"Oh, love-lee, love-lee," cried Maria Teresa softly as she looked at each new thing.

"And this is the cradle for our cradle roll," said Carol, stopping by a real little cradle with a tiny pink and white quilt. "See the little pockets that look like blankets? See the little paper babies in them?

"The babies have the names of our brothers and sisters who are too little to be in Sunday school. When someone has a new baby at his house, Sister Ruby writes its name on another paper baby and puts it in another pocket."

"Oh, da love-lee leetle bed," said Maria Teresa. She smoothed the tiny pink and white quilt and brushed some dust off the top of the cradle.

"The quilt is dusty too," said Carol, a bit ashamed that the cradle looked dirty to the stranger.

"Sister Ruby takes out the babies and washes the quilt sometimes. I guess she didn't see that it is not very clean anymore."

"Eet not-a matter," said Maria Teresa.

By this time, all the other children had come into the room. They sat quietly looking at the little Italian girl.

They had never seen a little girl quite like Maria Teresa. Her big black eyes looked out of a thin brown face. Her thick black hair was not in smooth braids like the other girls had. It curled around her face every which way.

Never had they seen such white teeth—maybe they just looked so white because her face was so brown. And there was something different about her dress. She wore a blue shawl instead of a sweater like all the other girls did. Besides that, she said her words so funny.

Carol led Maria Teresa to the bench at the table. She let the stranger go in first, then sat beside her.

The other boys and girls on the bench pushed down to the end, leaving an empty space between them and Maria Teresa.

Then Sister Ruby said, "Boys and girls, this is Maria Teresa Pinzarro. She has come across the ocean all the way from Italy. Let us sing our welcome song to her."

They sang "A Glad Welcome," but they did not act a bit glad as they sang. Some looked down and did not sing at all.

"Tank-a you, tank-a you," said Maria Teresa, with a happy smile. "Tank-a you for welcome to Sunny school."

Then Sister Ruby told the story of the Apostle Paul going to Rome. She asked the little Italian girl to point out on the wall map the town in Italy where she had lived.

"My fami-lee go to Roma two-tree time before we come to da America. I did not know da Apostala Paul-a go to Roma too."

Carol moved down the bench and Maria Teresa sat down at the end.

Someone laughed.

Another child said in a low voice, "Tank-a you, tank-a you."

Sister Ruby said quickly, "Now we will see if there are any new names for the cradle roll."

"Maria Teresa has some," spoke up Carol. "Go ahead, tell the names of your brothers and sister."

"I gotta tree names," said Maria Teresa, but she did not smile now. "Antonio and Carlos, my brudders, and Celestina, my leetle sister."

Sister Ruby got three new paper babies. While she wrote the new names, a boy whispered loudly, "Oh, love-lee, love-lee leetle brudders and sister."

Sister Ruby looked up sharply and shook her head at the boy. She gave the paper babies to Maria Teresa. The little girl went to the cradle and slipped them into the blanket pockets.

Then she sat down on a little chair nearby and said, "I sit-a here by da leetle bed. I do not need sit-a on bench with children who not like-a me."

"It is all right for you to sit there," said Sister Ruby. The teacher looked at the other children. Her eyes were sad but her mouth looked stern.

She went on with the lesson. The class looked down at their lesson books. They did not look back at the little stranger sitting all alone by the cradle with the pink and white quilt.

— Mary Ritchie Ward

The Missing Quilt

Part 2

The class was almost over when Carol cried suddenly, "Why, where is Maria Teresa?"

Now everyone turned around and looked. The little Italian had indeed gone.

"She slipped out the back door," guessed one of the boys.

"Do you know why she left?" asked the teacher in a **sorrowful** voice.

No one said anything.

"Then I will tell you why."

But before Sister Ruby could say another word, someone cried out, "The quilt is gone! The quilt from the cradle isn't there!"

The children jumped up and ran to look.

"That girl **snitched** it!"

"No wonder she ran away!"

"I thought she had a sneaky look about her."

"I bet she hid it under that shawl!"

"Carol, you must get it back for us!"

"And don't bring her to our class anymore!"

"She'll snitch something else!"

"That's why she wanted to sit back here by the cradle." Everyone talked at once, excited and angry.

"Children! Children!" Sister Ruby's voice sounded sharp and stern. "All of you sit down and listen to me!"

And they did.

"In our lesson the Apostle Paul went to Italy. There he told the people he met about Jesus who loves them. Today a little girl from Italy came to this class of children who already know about Jesus' love. What did she see or feel or hear of Jesus' love today?"

Sister Ruby kept on talking. Before she had stopped, some of the children were crying.

"Now before we **dismiss**, I want each of you to learn parts of three Bible verses. Two of them tell us what *charity* does. *Charity* means 'love.' I will write them on the board."

Sister Ruby wrote in big letters:

"Charity . . . is kind."
"Charity . . . thinketh no evil."
"I was a stranger and ye took me in."

All the children said the verses. All of them said they were sorry for the way they had treated Maria Teresa.

"I will tell her all about it," said Carol. "I will tell her you all want her to come back."

"One more thing," said the teacher. "If she comes back next Sunday, I may ask her about the quilt, or I may not. But I don't want any of you to say a word about it. We will let God work it out for us.

"But if she does not come back, I think you will know why."

✣   ✣   ✣   ✣   ✣

The next Sunday at starting time, everyone was there but Maria Teresa.

"I did not see her all week. I could not tell her that you all were sorry. She probably will never come back," Carol said.

"We will just have to start without her," said Sister Ruby.

"Oh, wait-a, wait-a, please," cried a voice, and in ran Maria Teresa, her black curls flying. "I'm leetle bit late. But-a I couldn't help it, Mees Teacher."

Then running to the cradle, Maria Teresa drew from under her shawl the pink and white quilt. How fresh and clean it looked.

"I take-a home for wash. Was leetle dirty last week.

My mama say I should-a not take-a quilt without tell-a you. But I want-a surprise so you like-a me. So I can come to your Sunny school.

"Dis I bring. See I make-a leetle pillow too, for da leetle bed. I take-a fedders from my pillow at home. And my mama make-a leetle lace pillow slip. She knows how to make-a fine lace like-a in Eetaly."

Maria Teresa held up a tiny pillow with a beautiful white lace slip.

The children crowded around as the girl spread the clean quilt in the little cradle, and placed the tiny pillow just right.

"See the little pillow. And lace, real lace!" they cried.

"You like-a?" asked the girl, smiling shyly.

"Oh, yes," cried all the class.

Then one of the girls raised her hand. "Sister Ruby, could we sing 'A Glad Welcome' to Maria Teresa again? I think we can do better than we did last Sunday."

—Mary Ritchie Ward

> *"And God created great whales."*
> – Genesis 1:21

Adventures Down Under

At birth, Young Blue was already bigger than most
other fully grown animals. He was a blue whale. Blue
whales are the biggest animals in the world. They are
not fish. They cannot breathe underwater. They can stay
underwater a long time, but must **eventually** come up
to the surface for air.

Mother Whale began teaching her baby from the
time he came into the world. At first, she pushed him
to the surface of the water for air. Then she stayed
close to him, watching over him and showing him
things he had to know. He found out how to use his
flukes, which are the ends of his flat tail. He moved
his flukes up and down to push himself through the
water. He followed his mother as she dived. When he
stayed underwater for ten or fifteen minutes, Young Blue
held his breath. Then he came to the surface and let out

a puff of moist air that rose like a fountain above his head.

After Young Blue learned to swim well, his mother took him far out into the ocean. There he saw many other whales. Some of them looked just like himself, but some looked quite different. He saw young dolphins that played about like puppies. He saw shiny black whales with square faces and sharp teeth. Young Blue and his mother joined a **pod** of blue whales that traveled together. This pod moved around the ocean looking for food.

For the first six or seven months of his life, Young Blue didn't have to look for his own food at all. When he was hungry, he bumped his mother with his big nose. She fed him milk just as a cow feeds her baby calf. Eventually he grew old enough to get food for himself. He learned to open his big jaws and take a huge mouthful of water full of tiny sea plants and animals. Then he strained out the food and swallowed it. He needed a lot of food because he was growing very fast.

The pod of whales moved on across the ocean looking for good feeding places. They found "meadows" on the surface of the water. In these places there were so many little plants and animals that the water took on different colors. At times it looked red or brown or green. The whales ate tons of food in each meadow. Then they moved on to other feeding places.

Young Blue traveled with the other whales from South America to Africa. They moved down along the coast of Africa, heading towards the cool waters near the South Pole. Eventually they found themselves swimming among great pieces of ice floating in the water. Penguins waddled about on the ice and **sleek** seals barked noisily. For weeks the pod of whales feasted in the cool waters where there was plenty of food.

As the season changed, Young Blue and the other whales moved again. Winter brought cold weather to the South Pole and the whales headed back to warmer waters.

Then Young Blue learned of the dangers from man. One day a whaling ship passed close to the pod. The hunters cut off the biggest whale from the pod. They chased it with a fast boat. The whale dived and stayed down as long as it could. But eventually it had to come up for air. Each time the hunters were waiting for it. Finally it grew too tired to dive any more. Then they killed it. The other whales swam away faster than the big whaling ship could travel.

A few days later the blue whales saw the fins of five killer whales cutting through the water toward them. They knew their lives were again in danger.

The big blue whales began to dive and swim away. Young Blue's mother stayed near him. One of the killer whales caught up with them. It headed for Young Blue.

The baby whale dived deep, but the killer came after him. It opened its huge jaws, showing its fierce teeth. It tried to bite Young Blue's face. Young Blue had no teeth to use in a fight with the killer whale. For a while it seemed that he didn't have a chance against his swift-moving enemy.

Then Young Blue's mother dived down from the surface. She swam between the killer and her baby. She twisted about and smashed her huge tail at the killer. The enemy swam to the surface for air but came back again, biting at the mother's flukes. The great blue whale twisted in pain. The killer moved around to attack her face. It came at her with its great jaws open. Young Blue's mother moved her huge body around and struck the killer with a mighty blow of her tail. The killer whale, **stunned** and helpless, rose to the surface of the water and lay there. Several other killer whales turned upon it, ready to eat it.

The young whale and his mother swam away as quickly as they could. They joined the pod, which moved on from that place of danger, looking for a sea meadow where they could rest and feed.

They came to the warm waters off the coast of Brazil, where Young Blue had been born. Some of the mother whales began looking for quiet places where they could have their babies. The other whales waited in a feeding place nearby until the mothers and their new babies could join them.

Then they all set out on a life of adventure down under the surface of the ocean just as Young Blue and his mother had done.

–adapted

"Jesus saith unto him, Go thy way; thy son liveth."

– John 4:50

Long-Distance Healing

46. So Jesus came again into Cana of Galilee, where he made the water wine. And there was a certain nobleman, whose son was sick at Capernaum.

47. When he heard that Jesus was come out of Judaea into Galilee, he went unto him, and besought him that he would come down, and heal his son: for he was at the point of death.

48. Then said Jesus unto him, Except ye see signs and wonders, ye will not believe.

49. The nobleman saith unto him, Sir, come down ere my child die.

50. Jesus saith unto him, Go thy way; thy son liveth. And the man believed the word that Jesus had spoken unto him, and he went his way.

51. And as he was now going down, his servants met him, and told him, saying, Thy son liveth.

52. Then enquired he of them the hour when he began to **amend**. And they said unto him, Yesterday at the seventh hour the fever left him.

53. So the father knew that it was at the same hour, in the which Jesus said unto him, Thy son liveth: and himself believed, and his whole house.

54. This is again the second miracle that Jesus did, when he was come out of Judaea into Galilee.

–John 4:46-54

> *"For every kind of beasts ... is tamed,*
> *and hath been tamed of mankind."*
>
> – James 3:7

Beaver Rescue

A True Story From 1940

One May day a baby beaver was born in a beaver lodge in Canada. The lodge was built in the waters of the Waskasoo Creek near Red Deer, Alberta.

For the first two or three weeks of life, he was one of a family of kits, cared for by his mother.

News that beavers were living near Red Deer brought lawbreakers to the area. Even though it was **illegal** to kill beavers, an unknown hunter began to trap many of the grown-up animals for their soft fur. In a short time only a few beavers remained. The babies' mother disappeared. The hungry young orphan kits were left to look after themselves.

Mr. Wallace Forbes lived near Waskasoo Creek. One

morning in early June, he found a baby beaver near his home. A bleeding wound cut across his back and another ugly slash opened one side. His hind legs hung almost useless.

The little animal's shoulder was also badly hurt. It seemed likely that a dog or a cat had found the baby beaver and nearly killed it, then left it on the creek bank to die.

Mr. Forbes carried the little fellow to the house. He and Mrs. Forbes cleaned its wounds. They put **ointment** and bandages on the large cuts on its back and side. They gently rubbed its shivering little body to warm it. Mrs. Forbes heated some sweetened milk. Then she held a spoon against the beaver's mouth and poured the milk slowly into the spoon. The hungry little animal began to lap the milk. He seemed nearly starved and lapped up every drop.

After he had eaten all he could hold, Mrs. Forbes placed him in a softly lined shoebox under the warm cookstove. Soon he fell fast asleep.

Mr. Forbes then paid a visit to the Royal Canadian Mounted Police. Since the government protects the beavers in Canada, it is illegal even to keep them. So Mr. Forbes went to tell the police what he had found. He told them he was afraid a dog or cat would kill the orphan beaver if he were turned loose on the creek again. He said he and Mrs. Forbes would look after the little animal if the Mounties would give them permission.

The police gave him permission, although no one thought the injured beaver kit would live very long.

However, the young beaver had found a good friend in Doris Forbes, the ten-year-old daughter of Mr. and Mrs. Forbes. Doris named her new pet "Mickey," and she became Mickey's nurse.

Three days later, strength began to return to Mickey's back. He began to walk again. A week later his wounds had almost healed. His shoulder remained stiff for a long time, but finally the stiffness disappeared and he was well again.

At first the Forbes family didn't know what to feed the baby beaver. He liked warm milk, of course, and they gave him lots of it. Then they offered him some lettuce, which he ate. Soon they found out that he liked grass shoots, leaves, and the **tender** bark from young trees.

In time Mickey learned to love almost any kind of fruit—strawberries, raspberries, oranges, and peaches. Garden peas became a favorite food, but Mickey never learned how to shell them. Doris always had to do the shelling for him.

Sometimes they gave him a special treat—an ice-cream cone. It made them laugh to watch Mickey eat a cone. When it melted and dripped down his coat, Mickey became very worried. He did not like to lose a single drop of the good cream, and he didn't want to get his fur coat dirty either.

Since beavers are water animals, Mr. Forbes made a small pond for Mickey in the backyard. The Forbes family also frequently took him to Sylvan Lake. There Mickey had plenty of room for swimming.

Because beavers are night-loving animals, Mickey slept most of the day. About five o'clock in the evening he woke up, ready for fun with Doris. At that time Mr. Forbes took a large pail down to the creek to get fresh water for the beaver. Mickey often waddled to the creekside with the family. He hurried home, though, when he saw Mr. Forbes carrying the water pail, for he knew what that meant.

Mickey lived in the empty garage. Doris kept a large pan of water there for him. Once a day Mr. Forbes cleaned out this pan and poured in the fresh pail of water. Mickey frequently climbed into the pail before it could be emptied into his pan, for he dearly loved a fresh drink.

Mrs. Forbes and Doris gave Mickey special little treats at this time of day. They fed him bread and milk, garden peas, and any fruits they had on hand. Mickey sat up straight on his hind legs, using his large flat tail as a **prop**. He held the food with his front paws and made a soft mewing sound as he ate.

Mickey ran about the house in the evening until the

family's bedtime. Then they took the beaver back to the garage. Since Mickey slept during the day, he spent most of the night "working like a beaver." He hauled boards all over the garage. Sometimes he put them in a pile that looked somewhat like a beaver lodge.

One morning during the first winter, Doris ran out to the garage and found Mickey wide awake. He was mewing loudly, so she carried him into the house. The temperature had dropped to nearly 50 degrees below zero, and they discovered that Mickey's hairless tail had frozen! Mickey wouldn't let any of the family help him. He quickly set to work himself, rubbing the frozen tail with his front paws. He rubbed it gently all day long, as patient as could be. He missed his sleep that day—but he saved his tail! After that, the family brought Mickey indoors during the coldest nights of winter.

By the time Mickey was fully grown, he measured more than three feet long. Doris no longer carried him in her arms, for he weighed over 75 pounds.

The Premier of Alberta gave Doris a special certificate of **ownership** for her pet. Sometimes she took Mickey to school to show the pupils what Canada's national animal looks like. The children liked to stroke his soft fur and look at his long, orange front teeth.

Once when Mrs. Forbes and Doris had left home for a two-week holiday, Mickey became very lonely. He wandered all over the house looking for his missing playmate. Finally he became quiet. Mr. Forbes went to find him. Mickey had found one of Doris' sweaters and was hugging it. Rocking back and forth, he stroked the sweater with one paw and mewed softly and happily to himself.

As for Doris—when other children told of their pet dogs and cats, canaries, or rabbits—she just smiled and insisted that she had the finest pet in all the world, Mickey the beaver.

—Kerry Wood

> *"Withhold not good from them to whom it is due,*
> *when it is in the power of thine hand to do it."*
>
> – Proverbs 3:27

My Quilt or Our House?

The very first thing Katy saw every morning was the crazy quilt on her bed. The neighbors at their old home back East had made it especially for her. It was a going-away gift.

"It is called a crazy quilt because the pieces are cut in crazy shapes," they said. "And they are sewed together any old way."

Katy never got tired of looking at the quilt. Often when she woke, she sat up and just looked at the quilt. Some of the pieces were of material like her own dresses. Some were patches like the dresses of her girl friends at her old home. Some were of material like Katy remembered their mothers wearing to church.

To Katy, her crazy quilt was the most beautiful thing in the whole new log house. She would hardly let anyone else even touch it. Especially not Father or big brother

David. Their hands might be dirty. And after Katy got the quilt, Mother never had to make her daughter's bed again.

This morning, after she had dressed, Katy took her time making her bed. She loved to smooth the beautiful quilt over it.

In the middle of the part that covered the pillow was a red square that had her name and the date sewed into it. Katy especially enjoyed putting that red patch in the middle of her pillow just so.

Then she heard David downstairs telling Mother of a rainstorm he saw coming. When Katy got downstairs, the kitchen was **deserted**. Mother and David were outside looking at the sky over the woods beyond the pasture. A black cloud was rolling higher and higher.

"That isn't a rain cloud," cried Mother in alarm. "That's smoke! The forest is on fire!

"Katy, run to the mill and tell Father. Perhaps he and the other men haven't seen it!

"David, we must take all our buckets and tubs and big kettles to the well and fill them with water. We will need plenty if we are going to save our house!"

Katy ran. She knew how quickly a forest fire could spread. As she ran, she imagined the flames leaping from tree to tree—getting nearer and nearer to the house. By the time she got to the mill at the river, she could smell the smoke.

"Father! A fire! The woods is on fire!" she screamed, as she burst through the mill door.

In a minute the mill was deserted. Father and the other men dashed out to look at the dark cloud slowly rising above the trees.

"Shovels, axes, buckets! Everyone grab something," Father shouted. "Thank God there is no wind. Maybe we can dig a ditch in the pasture behind the house and save it!"

In no time the men were running toward the house with Katy panting far behind them.

David was drawing water from the well as fast as he could. The washtubs were full and he was filling buckets and kettles.

"What can we do to help?" cried Mother when Father arrived.

"Get your blankets and quilts. Soak them in the tubs and spread them on the house roof. If we can keep sparks from setting fire to the **shingles**, we may save the house! The men and I are going to the pasture to dig a fire ditch!"

The men left on the run with their axes and shovels. Mother ran to the barn for the ladder.

"David," asked Katy, when she had arrived, "how can a ditch stop a forest fire?"

"It won't be a real ditch. It is just a wide strip of turned-over soil. When the fire gets to that strip there won't be anything to burn, so it will go out."

"Oh, I see," said Katy.

Then Mother arrived, dragging the ladder. She and David leaned it against the back of the house.

"Now, Katy, help bring out the covers," Mother instructed as she hurried to the house.

Katy followed in alarm. A great fear clutched her heart. "Not my quilt!" she whispered as she ran. "They can't soak my quilt and put it on that dirty roof to get burned up!"

"You get all the ones upstairs," instructed Mother. "Throw them down the steps. I'll get the ones down here."

Katy ran upstairs. She got the blankets and **comforters** from David's room and threw them down the steps. She got the quilts and blankets from the big chest in her room and threw them down the steps. But she did not touch her crazy quilt.

When she ran downstairs, she saw Mother going out the door with her arms piled high with covers. Katy scooped up an armful and followed.

As soon as Mother arrived at the well, David grabbed a quilt. He stuffed it into a tub of water. When it was soaked through, he dragged it to the house and up the ladder, dripping all the way.

The **sodden** quilt was almost too heavy for him to handle, soaked as it was. But he struggled with it up the sloping roof. He spread it across the peak and

smoothed it out. Then he came down to the top of the ladder. Mother waited there with another dripping blanket.

And so they worked, while the smoke grew thicker and the fire burned closer. Katy soaked the covers. Mother carried them up the ladder. David spread them on the roof.

All the time, as Katy drew water from the well and stuffed covers into the tubs, she was glad her beautiful quilt had not been soaked and dragged across the muddy ground.

David had just spread the last dripping comforter on the roof when Father and the men arrived from the pasture. **Soot**, ashes, and dirt covered them from head to foot. Their burning eyes streamed with tears.

"The smoke is too thick. We have done all we could. Only God knows if the ditch will stop the fire," gasped

Father. "Let us take a minute to ask God to protect us. Then you men better go and see about your own homes across the river."

Father prayed a short prayer, then the other men hurried away. Father sat down, breathing hard.

He looked toward the house. "You have done a good job. There is just that one place that needs to be covered yet. If sparks caught the shingles there, all your work would be for nothing."

"We've used all the covers," said Mother. "And we have spread them out as well as we could."

Katy said nothing. She wasn't, she just *wasn't,* going to let them spoil her beautiful crazy quilt.

But then she looked toward the forest. Now she could see the leaping flames and hear the roar of the fire. She could hear the crackling of burning branches and the crash of falling trees.

Sparks flew over the house. When they lit on the wet quilts, they instantly went out. Katy looked at the one bare spot.

Suddenly she said, "I left my-my-my crazy quilt in the house. I'll go and get it."

Katy began to cry as she ran to the house. But she dragged the beautiful quilt off her bed. Just as she came out the door, she heard Father shout, "The shingles have caught fire there on that bare spot!"

Mother snatched the crazy quilt from Katy and

stuffed it into the nearest tub. Father dragged it through the mud as he dashed for the ladder. Up he went and slung the quilt over the blaze that had started on the roof.

The fire went out. Then he spread the whole quilt over the bare spot. He came slowly down the ladder, almost too worn out to move.

David and Mother had been running here and there with buckets of water, putting out little fires that had started in the dry grass.

Father called to them through the choking smoke, "We had better head for the river. I can't see if the fire has jumped our ditch or not."

At the same time David cried, "Rain! I felt a drop of rain!"

Everyone had been so busy fighting the fire that they hadn't noticed the clouds building up in the west. Soon they all felt the drops. A few at first, then more and more, until the rain came in a wonderful, cooling downpour.

The family stood with their blackened faces turned to the sky. No one knew or cared whether their faces were wet with rain or tears of thankfulness.

It rained hard for over an hour. The family waited in the house, too soaked, tired, and dirty to do anything but thank God for saving their home.

Then the sun came out bright and hot. Father and David went up on the roof and threw down the quilts and blankets. Every one of them was sodden and dirty black from the smoke and ashes that had fallen on the roof. But not one of them had a single burned place—except the crazy quilt. It had a big black hole where the fire on the roof had burned it.

Katy began to cry when she saw it. "My quilt! My beautiful quilt! It will never be nice again!"

"Never mind," said Mother. "It can be washed. And I will get some new material and make a lovely piece to cover the hole. Then we can remember that your crazy quilt saved our house."

And that is just what they did. They covered the burned hole with a bright patch. On it were the words, "The Fire of 1868."

It took Mother and Katy many days to wash all the quilts and blankets and comforters that had covered the roof. It was a long time until they were clean and dry and back in the closets and chests where they belonged.

It took especially long before the crazy quilt with its new patch was back on Katy's bed.

The new piece fit in just fine with the other crazy-shaped patches. But every time Katy looked at it, she couldn't help thinking, "If I had taken my quilt out to begin with, it would not have gotten burned at all."

–*Ruth Holbrook*

The SOS Adventure Team

Paul and Don Fisher lived on Red Oak Island. Many people had built summer homes on the west side of the island. A **ferry** brought people and supplies from the mainland. Then a little train took them from the dock at the east end on across the island.

The ferryboat and the train were very busy in the summer. But in the winter most of the summer people went to their homes on the mainland. Then the ferry ran only four times a day, and the train carried supplies only once a week.

The boys' father ran the steam **locomotive** with its few cars, so the family lived near the east end of the island all year. Paul and Don rode the ferry to attend school on the mainland.

In winter the quiet island might have been dull for Paul and Don. But in the woods north of the train tracks lived Big Jerry. He was a trapper who, before he came to the island, had made his living hunting bears in Canada. He told wonderful stories when the boys came to visit. Sometimes Jerry invited them to supper, and that was the most fun of all. The trapper knew how to cook. He fried bacon in long strips without letting it curl up. Then he fried potatoes and eggs. He said, "Eggs make you smart."

The boys always worked as a team. At Jerry's, Paul pumped water at the kitchen pump for supper. Don got the chairs and set the table. And they always washed the dishes together afterwards.

The boys secretly wished they could sleep at Jerry's sometime. They thought sleeping in his spare bedroom would be the greatest fun! The big bed was made of log posts and planks. The mattress was a layer of thick, furry, black bearskins. But the big trapper had never invited them. Probably he did not realize how they would enjoy it. If they stayed at his cabin until after dark, he always walked home with them.

Then one night something happened. Don and Paul had spent the evening with Big Jerry. He had walked home with them as usual. Daddy and Mother met the three at the door. Daddy said he and Mother had been called away suddenly. They would be gone a week.

At once Jerry said, "Could the boys stay with me? I would be glad to have them."

"That would be wonderful," said Daddy. "Then they won't miss any school. We'll not worry about the boys if they are with you."

Paul and Don were delighted. At last they would get to sleep at Jerry's. They got their clothes and school things together and said good-bye to their parents. Then they went back with Jerry to his cozy cabin.

After supper that night, Jerry told them about a baby bear he had once found caught in a sugar barrel. He told about taming the bear and teaching it tricks. He told other tales of his bear-hunting days. Then the boys snuggled into the big bed with the bearskin mattress.

The next morning when Jerry woke the boys, it was snowing hard outside. "I'll cook extra eggs for everybody," said Jerry. "They'll keep you warm and make you smart too."

Bundled up in boots, coats, caps, and **mufflers**, the boys set out for the dock and the ferryboat that would take them across to the mainland to school.

When Paul and Don climbed aboard the ferry, the captain called, "Well, you're a tough team! I thought you wouldn't make it today! Better be sure to catch the three-o'clock ferry home. I won't make the five-o'clock run over here this afternoon if this storm keeps up."

That afternoon the boys left school early and caught the three-o'clock ferry to the island. As it pulled away from the dock, they felt as if they were chugging off into nothing. The swirling snow made a thick white wall around the boat. They were glad when the ferry made it to the island safely.

Pulling their caps low and snuggling into their mufflers, Paul and Don headed into the storm. Snow had covered the trail, so they followed the telephone poles along the railroad tracks.

"I know Jerry will have a roaring fire and a path dug to the railroad track for us," said Paul.

But the pair found no path, so they struck off toward the cabin through the deepening snow. Even when they got close to Jerry's cabin, they saw no footprints. No smoke curled from the chimney. Something was wrong!

Both boys burst into the cabin. The room felt icy cold. Big Jerry lay on the floor with firewood scattered all around.

"Jerry! Jerry!" cried Paul and Don together.

The trapper groaned and opened his eyes. "I tripped," he said. "My head hurts. I think something is wrong with my right leg. And I'm cold."

The two boys brought several bearskins from the bedroom. Jerry dragged himself onto one. They covered him with another.

"Don't try to get up, Jerry," said Paul. "We will think of something to do."

"You figure out what to do, Paul, while I make a fire

in the stove and get this cabin warm," said Don.

"The ferry won't come back from the mainland anymore today, and probably not tomorrow, if this storm keeps up," said Paul. "We'll have to telephone the Coast Guard and tell them what's happened. They'll send the **cutter**. There's a doctor on board."

"Right!" said Don. He tried the telephone. "It's dead. The wires must be down. Now what?" he asked in a worried tone.

"I don't know," said Paul. "Let me think."

In a minute he said, "I know! We'll send SOS in code. Three short, three long, three short!"

"Three long and short what?" asked Don.

"Three long and short whistles on the train engine if we can get up enough steam in the boiler to blow the whistle," said Paul. "We'll keep sending SOS till the Coast Guard hears it and comes."

Paul and Don made Jerry as comfortable as possible. The stove had begun to throw out good heat. After making sure the fire was safe, they hurried out into the storm. They fought their way through the blinding snow to the engine house.

As they opened the door of the engine house, Don panted, "It's a mighty good thing Dad keeps the engine under roof with plenty of dry wood."

The boys climbed up into the cab of the locomotive. Using the wood their father had left, Don started a fire in the firebox to heat the water in the boiler.

Paul said, "It won't take much steam to blow the whistle, but it's got to be boiling."

Don said nothing. Slowly he fed piece after piece of wood into the firebox. Paul watched the steam **gauge**. The minutes seemed like hours before the water began to get hot. Slowly the gauge inched up and up to the boiling point.

At last Paul said, "I'm almost afraid to try it. But I think she'll whistle now."

"Well, I'll try it," said Don. He jerked the whistle cord three times.

The whistle sounded three short, clear sounds. *Toot, toot, toot.* Then three long blasts. *Toooot! Toooot! Toooot!* Then three short ones again.

Over and over the boys blew the signal, three short, three long, three short. They shoved more wood into the firebox before signaling again. Over and over and over. But they heard no answering sound.

"The wind is wrong," Paul said at last. "And we don't know where the cutter is. It may be answering our signals. But we can't hear it."

Just then, they heard a hoarse whistle that they knew came from the Coast Guard cutter. It sounded quite close to the island.

"Get down to the dock," Paul ordered. "Tell them what's wrong. I'll stay here till the fire dies down."

Don hurried into the storm, following the poles along the tracks. How glad he was to see the Coast Guard cutter at the dock when he got there. The captain put out his head and shouted, "What's the trouble?"

"Big Jerry has fallen and hurt himself—badly!" Don shouted back. "He needs help."

Every man on the cutter knew Big Jerry. The doctor and three others followed Don to Jerry's cabin.

The doctor examined Big Jerry. Then he said, "You have a bad bump on the head and a broken leg. The bones are in place, though. All I can do is **splint** it for you tonight."

The doctor set to work putting a splint on the broken leg. The other coastguardsmen began to bring in wood. They built a fire in the fireplace and added wood to the stove.

As the doctor worked, he said, "This boy, here, was clever to think of that whistle to get help for you, Jerry. We knew that train whistle as soon as we heard it."

Don said, "I didn't think of the whistle. Paul did. He's staying with the engine until the fire dies down."

"The boys make a real team," Jerry said. "Paul plans. Don makes the plans work. One is just as smart as the other. They eat lots of eggs. That's why they're so smart."

At last the doctor got up and said, "There! You will have to stay quiet, Jerry, till we can move you out of here.

It may be a day or two. But I'll be back in the morning to have a look at you, if the snow doesn't get too deep."

Paul arrived in time to hear the doctor's last words. "You mean Jerry will be all right?" he asked. "And Don and I can take care of him for sure?"

The doctor didn't answer right away. He was helping the coastguardsmen lift Jerry carefully onto the couch near the fireplace.

When Jerry was settled, the doctor answered Paul's question. "Jerry will have to stay here until this storm blows over. Then we will get him out to the hospital. But he'll be all right as long as he stays quiet and doesn't move that leg."

The doctor smiled at the boys. "You two can't go to school anyway. So you can look after your friend. Give him this medicine every four hours and keep the fires going night and day."

The room was getting warm and cozy by now.

One of the coastguardsmen looked around and said, "I wish we could stay here too. It would be a lot better than going out again on a night like this."

The doctor said, "But of course we can't. We have to be on duty for other folks who might be in trouble."

"Thanks for the rescue," said Big Jerry.

"You are welcome," said the doctor. "Going to the rescue is our business. These boys are the ones you need to thank. They are quite a team."

As the coastguardsmen went out the door, one of them turned and said, "If you need help again, fellows, just give us a whistle."

–Gertrude C. Warner

In the story you just read, Paul and Don didn't have
time to do what the children in this poem like to do.

White Fields

In the wintertime we go
Walking in the fields of snow;

   Where there is no grass at all;
   Where the top of every wall,

Every fence and every tree,
Is as white as white can be.

   Pointing out the way we came,
   —Every one of them the same—

All across the fields there be
Prints in silver filigree;

   And our mothers always know,
   By the footprints in the snow,

Where it is the children go.

—James Stephens

Snoopy Learns About Beeswax

As Carl came into the house, Mother looked up from a letter she was reading. "Well, Son, how do you like your new school? How does it feel to be in third grade?"

"It seems funny to have five grades in one room. There aren't as many children in those five grades as there were in my second-grade room last year.

"It is nice to have big boys and girls to play with at recess. Only they say funny things sometimes."

"I told you the children here will talk a little differently from what you are used to. But I guess you sound funny to them too. I'm sure it will not take long to get used to their way of saying things."

"I guess so," said Carl. Then he asked, "Mother, what is beeswax?"

"Beeswax?" said Mother. "You must have had a science lesson today. You know what beeswax is. It is what bees make the **cells** with. They make cells for honey and cells for the baby bees and—"

But Carl began talking again. "Who is your letter from? It must be from Grandma. No one else knows our new address yet. What does she say? Is she coming to see us soon?"

"Carl—," began Mother.

But Carl did not hear because he had begun looking at the pile of mail on the table. He picked up a small brown package.

"Oh, here is a little package for Daddy. I wonder what is in it. Did he send for something? Do you think he'd care if I opened it for him? It is from R. J. Rice Company." Carl gave the package a shake or two. "It does not sound like rice. I guess that is just the name of the company."

He gave the package two or three more shakes. "It is so light, it can't have much of anything in it. May I open it, Mother? Daddy won't care."

"Carl," said Mother again.

But Carl was not listening. "Oh, here is a letter to Betty. It is from Pam. I wonder how those two girls are going to like writing letters instead of talking on the telephone all the time like they did before we moved away.

"This envelope is so thin I can almost read what she wrote." Carl held the envelope to the light and read slowly, ". . . not—go—to—the . . ."

"Carl, put that letter down and listen to me," said Mother sharply.

Carl put the letter on the table and looked at Mother. She said, "Did you forget what we talked about just before we moved here?"

Carl got red in the face. "You mean about—about—about what the children called me at school?"

"Yes, that is what I mean. What did I say?"

"You said no one in this school will know about the name."

"And what else did I say?"

"You said if I didn't like being called Snoopy, I should stop *being* **snoopy**."

"And what else?"

"You said that when we moved here I could put a stop to the name if I stopped being snoopy."

"Well," said Mother, "you have been home from school about fifteen minutes. In that time you have asked who my letter was from. You asked what Grandmother said. You shook Daddy's package and wanted to open it. And you tried to read what Pam had written to Betty. Are you really trying not to be snoopy?"

"But, Mother, this is not school. At home it doesn't matter. Anyway, I'm *interested* in things. What is wrong with being interested in things?"

"You and I have talked about this before, Carl. You know it is all right to be interested in some things. God wants you to be interested in your schoolwork. He wants you to be interested in His world around us. He wants you to be interested in the Bible and in trying to please Him and in making others happy.

"But He does not want you to be snooping into other people's business. You know being snoopy does not make others happy. That is why the children called you Snoopy last year."

Carl said nothing.

"You even know the Bible verse that teaches us not to be a busybody in other people's business. A busybody is someone who makes himself busy finding out other people's business. You keep on snooping into things that are none of your business. Don't you care if people call you Snoopy?"

"Yes, I care!" cried Carl, almost in tears. "I hate it! I hate it! I'm glad I'm not going to that school anymore!"

"The children at this school could call you Snoopy too, or something worse."

"But this is a Christian school. Children in a Christian school should not call names," said Carl.

"No, they shouldn't," agreed Mother. "But should children in a Christian school be busybodies? You seem more interested in the other children doing right than in doing right yourself."

"I can't help it if I am interested in other people's business, can I?"

"No," said Mother, "you can't help wondering about something that looks or sounds interesting. But you don't need to *keep* thinking and wondering about it. That is when you start asking snoopy questions like you did about my letter. That is when you start doing snoopy things like shaking Daddy's package and trying to read Betty's letter.

"When something is not your business, put it out of your mind. Think about something else."

"But I like to find out about interesting things," cried Carl. "I can't help thinking and wondering."

"If you can't keep yourself from *being* snoopy, do you think you can keep the children from calling you Snoopy?" asked Mother.

Again Carl said nothing.

"Maybe we have talked about this long enough," said Mother. "Tell me about your science lesson. Didn't the teacher tell you what beeswax is?"

"We didn't have science. It was one of those funny things a big boy said. His name is Bruce. I don't know all the children's names yet, but I remember his because he has braces on his teeth. Brace and Bruce are almost alike. That's how I remember his name."

"What did he say?" asked Mother.

"Well, we were eating lunch outside. I asked him how much his braces cost."

"Carl! You didn't!" exclaimed Mother.

"What was wrong with that? One of the girls had said she needed braces, but they didn't have enough money. I wondered how much braces cost, so I just asked him."

"And what did he say?"

"That was when he said that funny thing. He said, 'None of your beeswax.'"

Mother smiled, then began to laugh. "We used to say that when I was a little girl. I haven't heard anyone say that for years and years!"

"But what does it mean?" cried Carl. "One of the girls said the same thing when I asked what was in a little box she had on her desk. 'None of your beeswax.' That doesn't make any sense!" Carl was getting cross.

Mother had stopped laughing. She was not even smiling anymore. "I'll tell you what it means, Carl," she said. "It means, 'None of your *business*.' And those children were right. It is none of your business what people pay for the things they buy. It is none of your business what others have in their boxes or desks or pockets or notebooks or letters."

"But I just wondered," said Carl in a small voice.

"It is time for you to stop wondering about things that are none of your business," said Mother. "Another day like this one and the children in this school will begin calling you Snoopy, just like they did at the other school."

"Oh, no, Mother. I don't want them to do that," Carl cried, almost in tears again. "I thought in a Christian school they wouldn't call names. Can't you call the teacher and tell her not to let them call me names?"

"Carl," said Mother. "Why are you thinking what the school children should or should not do? Why are you thinking about what I and the teacher should do? This is *your* problem. *You* are the one who is the busybody. Why don't you think about what *you* might do?"

Carl was quiet for a long, long time. At last he said, "I don't want to be a busybody, Mother. Really I don't. Can you help me not to be snoopy anymore? Not at school and not at home."

Mother put her arm around Carl. "The first thing to do is to ask God to help you. Then I think Daddy and I will need to think of a plan that will make you hate to be snoopy as badly as you hate to be called Snoopy. And I will call your teacher and tell her the plan and ask her to help you at school like we are helping you at home."

"Oh, Mother," was all Carl could say.

Carl never told anyone what Mother and Daddy planned. At first there were many tears. Most of them were in Carl's eyes. But sometimes they were in Daddy's eyes and sometimes in Mother's.

One day, weeks later, when the children were walking in from the playground, Bruce put his hand on Carl's shoulder. "Say, Carl," he said, smiling behind his braces, "I am sure glad you moved here. At first I thought you were going to be a real snoopy. But I was wrong, because you mind your own beeswax better than anyone in this whole school."

–Ruth K. Hobbs

What keeps the busy bee from being a busybody?

How Doth the Little Busy Bee

How doth the little busy bee
   Improve each shining hour
And gather honey all the day
   From every passing flower!

How skillfully she builds her cell;
   How neat she spreads the wax!
And labors hard to store it well
   With the sweet food she makes.

–Isaac Watts

The Elm Avenue Mystery

Jan and her sister Maggie sat on the front porch steps talking about the **lopsided** *B*'s, *P*'s, and *S*'s written in chalk on the sidewalk. Overnight the mysterious letters had appeared in front of almost every house on Elm Avenue.

"Who do you think the chalker is, Maggie?"

Maggie shrugged. "All I want to know is why anyone would be doing it. There is an *S* at some houses and a *B* at ours. Some houses have a *P*.

"Grandpa says in the old days tramps used to make chalk marks on farm gates to tell other tramps if the people at that place were nice or not. But there are no tramps around here now."

"I know," said Jan. She **pondered** the Elm Avenue mystery for a minute. "What do you suppose those letters stand for? If we knew what they meant, we could guess who the chalker is."

"That's right," said Maggie. "Let's think who on Elm Avenue would do something strange like this. There's old Mr. Tullen. People say there is something funny about him. I wouldn't be surprised if he did it."

"But he has a letter on his walk. He wouldn't mess up his own pavement, would he?"

"I guess not, unless he put one at his place to throw us off the track. Strange people do strange things, you know. How about Mrs. Simms? They say she turned her neighbor's rainwater barrel over because she said it was drawing mosquitoes. There is no letter at her house."

"Aw, come on, Maggie. I know she is sour. But how could she be sour on almost everyone for four blocks? It can't be her. Look how old she is. I'd say it's someone like Dick Stone."

"That's a good guess, Jan. He always makes trouble at school, and we saw him walking by here yesterday afternoon, remember? But I'd say playing tricks with chalk is too tame for Dick. He'd dream up something a lot worse than that."

"Maybe the letters are his secret mark at houses where he plans to do something mean—you know, rob them or something."

"That would be more like him," agreed Maggie.

"Girls!" Daddy's voice came through the open window behind them.

Jan and Maggie looked at each other.

"What?" asked Jan in a small voice.

"Come here."

The girls went into the house and stood before their father. Both felt guilty for some reason, but they could not have explained why.

"What were you girls doing?" asked Daddy kindly.

"We were just talking about the letters someone has chalked on the walk in front of people's houses," explained Jan.

"What do you know about them?"

"Nothing, really," admitted Maggie. "That is the mystery. We were trying to think who on Elm Avenue could be doing it."

"Yes, I heard you," said Daddy. "But it made me think of several other things besides the mystery. I thought about some Bible verses. One was, 'Charity thinketh no evil.' Another one talks about 'evil **surmising**,' and the third one I thought about was, 'speak evil of no man.'

"When you repeat **critical** things you have heard about Mr. Tullen and Mrs. Simms, you are speaking evil of them. When you imagine evil things that Dick Stone might have done, you are thinking evil and surmising evil. Isn't that correct?"

"Yes," said the girls together in voices hardly above a whisper.

"What do Mr. Tullen and Mrs. Simms and Dick

Stone have to do with this Elm Avenue mystery, anyway?"

"Nothing that we know of," admitted Jan with a quick look at Maggie. "We were just thinking about who might be writing those letters."

"Yes, thinking and imagining evil and talking," said Daddy. "What is so terrible about chalk letters on a sidewalk? They don't hurt you or anyone else. The person who put them there has done no wrong. Who are the guilty ones? Who are the ones who have been doing wrong?"

Jan and Maggie looked at the floor and said nothing.

"You may go now, but I want you both to watch your thoughts. You have pondered on this mystery until you are imagining evil things and repeating evil things about your neighbors. If you think *kind* thoughts, you won't be so critical of others.

"Find out about those letters, if you want to, but go hunt for facts instead of sitting on the porch letting your imaginations run away with you."

Jan and Maggie went out. They were ashamed of themselves. Daddy's scolding had somehow taken the fun out of the mystery. They didn't feel like talking about it anymore.

The girls stood on the walk and looked up and down the street. Far down at the end of the avenue, they saw a bike with training wheels. It was heavily loaded with newspapers. A small boy was riding it, wobbling in a crisscross pattern from one side of the street to the other.

"Isn't that Teddy Turner?" asked Jan.

"Yes. He is our new paper boy," answered Maggie.

"He looks too little to be hauling that load. It's a wonder they give a job to a little fellow like that." Jan felt sorry for the boy.

The girls went back to the porch steps and sat down. They watched Teddy come up the street delivering papers to different houses. He tossed a paper onto Mr. Tullen's porch. Then he rode across the street and climbed the steps to the porch of the next house. There he put a paper inside the screen door. Next, he stopped and came up the walk toward the girls, carrying their newspaper.

"Just give it to us," said Jan. "You don't need to put it on the back porch today."

"Thanks," said Teddy. "That saves me some time." He returned to his bike and went on zig-zagging along Elm Avenue.

A week later, people on Elm Avenue still pondered the mysterious letters. Some people called the police, who told them the letters didn't hurt anyone. Others called the newspaper and were told it wasn't important enough to print. People washed the chalk off, but the lopsided *B*'s and *P*'s and *S*'s were always back the next morning.

Maggie and Jan couldn't forget the mystery. On the way home from the store one evening, Jan said, "We have heard many crazy ideas about how the letters get on the sidewalk, but you and I better stick to facts like Daddy said. Why don't we get up early in the morning and see if we can catch someone putting the letters back on the walk."

"Yes, let's," said Maggie. Suddenly she grabbed Jan's arm and pointed toward someone kneeling on the sidewalk halfway down the block. "Look there! Maybe that's the chalker," she whispered.

"Let's walk down that way and see what he is doing."

As the girls came near, the figure stood up. It was Teddy Turner. He held a scrub brush and a bucket of water.

"Whatever are you doing?" asked Jan.

"Washing my letters off the pavement. I don't need them anymore."

"So *you* are the mysterious chalker! You have had the whole neighborhood upset for more than a week."

"I kind of figured I did. I had to put most of the marks back every evening."

"Why did you put them there in the first place?" asked Maggie.

"The newspaper gave me my job only on **trial**. They thought I was too little." Teddy smiled. "I proved I could do it. Every customer was happy with the way I delivered his paper. Now I'm a regular paper boy."

Jan and Maggie followed the little boy to the next lopsided letter and watched as he began to scrub at it.

"What did the letters stand for?" asked Jan.

"They told me where the customer wanted his paper. I asked all of them where they wanted me to put it. Some wanted it behind the screen door. So I put *S* in front of that house. If they wanted it on the front porch I put *P* at that house. Your folks want it at the back door, so I put *B* on your walk. That's what the letters meant."

Jan and Maggie just stared at Teddy.

"Is that all?" gasped Jan. "Here we were thinking—thinking ..."

"Thinking what?" asked Teddy.

"I'm too ashamed to tell you," said Jan. "It wasn't

anything about you, though. It was just something we imagined about some people who had nothing to do with it. Were we ever off the track, Maggie!"

"Were we ever!" exclaimed Maggie. "Come on, Jan, let's go home. I want to tell Daddy we solved the Elm Avenue mystery by learning the facts, just like he told us to do."

–Jane K. Priewe

Daddy helped Jan and Maggie see a better way than imagining evil of others. This poem tells the best ways to handle things you hear about others.

The Better Way

If anything unkind you hear
About someone you know, my dear,
Do not, I pray you, it repeat
When you that "someone" chance to meet,
For such news has a leaden way
Of clouding o'er a sunny day.

But if you something pleasant hear
About someone you know, my dear,
Make haste—to make great haste 'twere well,
To her or him the same to tell;
For such news has a golden way
Of lighting up a cloudy day.

—Author Unknown

Which verse of this poem do you think Jan and Maggie needed the most?

If You Were

If you were busy being kind,
Before you knew it, you would find
You'd soon forget to think 'twas true
That someone was unkind to you.

If you were busy being glad
And cheering people who are sad,
Although your heart might ache a bit,
You'd soon forget to notice it.

If you were busy being good
And doing just the best you could,
You'd not have time to blame some man
Who's doing just the best he can.

If you were busy being right,
You'd find yourself too busy quite
To criticize your neighbor long
Because he's busy being wrong.

—Author Unknown

> *"When pride cometh, then cometh shame:
> but with the lowly is wisdom."*
>
> – Proverbs 11:2

All About the Ocean

Jean was excited. Her cousin, Cathy, was coming to visit. Cathy had never been to the ocean. The ocean was just across the yard and down the cliff from Jean's house. You had to go down fifty wide steps to get to the bottom of the cliff. Then, there you were on the beach.

"I will tell Cathy all about the ocean," Jean said to Mother and Daddy. "I guess she doesn't even know what a seagull is or the names of any of the shells. I guess she doesn't know about high **tide** and low tide."

"Maybe not," said Daddy.

The first thing Cathy said when she came, was, "Oh, Jean, I hope you know all about the ocean. I don't know anything. I need you to tell me about lots of things, because when school starts I must give a report. We must write a report about something we did this summer. I am going to write about the ocean. I'm

322

counting on you to give me all the information I need."

"All right," said Jean happily. "I know all about the ocean. I will tell you everything."

"I brought a notebook along," said Cathy. "I'm going to write down the information you give me. Then I'll be all set to write my report when school starts."

The first day the girls played on the beach all day. They did not think about school reports. They walked along and let the waves wash around their feet. They waded out and jumped over the waves as they rolled in to the shore.

Far back on the beach they built a sand castle. They had to go down to the ocean with their pails to get water so they could wet the sand and pack it.

"Tomorrow let's make our castle bigger yet," said Cathy, as they started up the fifty wide steps to the house at supper time.

The next morning when the girls got to the bottom of the cliff, Cathy cried, "Where is our sand castle? It's gone!"

Sure enough, a smooth stretch of white sand covered the place where the castle had been.

"The tide came in last night and washed it away," said Jean. "I was afraid it would."

"You mean the water came way up here?" asked Cathy in amazement. "You remember how far we had to walk to get water to pack the sand. The ocean was way down there."

"But the tide was going out then," said Jean. "Last night it came in. That's something to put in your report, Cathy—about high tide and low tide."

"I am going to get my notebook. That's interesting information," said Cathy. She ran up the fifty wide steps to the house among the pine trees on the cliff.

Jean watched her go. "Now I can tell her all about the ocean," she said to herself with a satisfied smile.

When Cathy came back, the girls sat on the bottom step.

"The title of my report is going to be "All About the Ocean." How do you spell *ocean*?"

"I don't know for sure," said Jean. *"O-s-h-u-n,* I think."

Cathy wrote it down. "That doesn't look right," she said. "But we can ask Aunt Nan when we get back to the house.

"Now tell me all about the tides." Cathy wrote "Tides" at the top of the first page.

"Well, the waves come in for a while every day. And after a while they start to go out again. At high tide the water comes up to where our castle was. At low tide it is way down there where it is now."

"What makes the waves do that?" asked Cathy next. "They don't do that on the lake at home."

"Well, I'm not sure," said Jean. "I heard Daddy talk about the pull of the moon, or the sun, or the earth, or something. I really don't know what makes the tides."

"You said the tide was going out when we were building our sand castle. But the waves were coming in all the time. How could the tide be going out if the waves were coming in?"

"I don't know," said Jean. "I never thought about that. It's just the way it does. That's all I know."

"We'll ask Uncle Benny when we get back to the house," said Cathy. She had not written anything under "Tides."

She turned a page in her notebook. She wrote "Birds" at the top. "Now tell me about the birds. They are so different from the birds I see at home. I guess those biggest ones we see flying by all the time are seagulls, aren't they?"

"Yes, those bigger birds are seagulls," said Jean. She was glad to stop talking about tides.

"But I want to know the names of the different kinds," said Cathy. "I can't be satisfied to say I saw seagulls. I want to list the kinds of seagulls I saw.

"Look, there is one with a black head. But most of them have white heads. And most of them have gray backs. But look at that one over there. He is bigger than the others. And he is black on the back. What kind is he?"

"I don't know," said Jean. "They are just seagulls. Mother's bird book can tell you the names of the different kinds. We can ask her when we go back."

Then Cathy said, "How about those little birds running on the shore down there close to the water? What kind are they?"

"They are sandpipers," said Jean.

"But they are not all the same kind. Some are grayish white. And some are more tan. I want their real names for my report. My teacher won't be satisfied unless I give real information."

"I don't know their real names. They all look about the same to me," said Jean. "Maybe we can find them in the bird book."

Then she said, "Do you want to walk on the beach and look for shells? I know the names of lots of shells— clams and pectens and-and-and—I can't think of them all."

"All right," said Cathy. She turned the page in her notebook. "I'll make a list of all the shells you know." She had not written anything under "Birds." Now she wrote "Shells" at the top of the page.

Most of the shells on the beach were broken. But Jean soon found a clam shell that was not broken.

"Here is a clam shell," she said, showing it to Cathy.

Cathy looked at it. "You mean a clam lived in that? How could it?"

"I don't know. But I know this is a clam shell. Daddy told me," said Jean.

Cathy took the clam shell in her hand. "No animal could live in this. It would fall out. The shell is just like a flat saucer."

Suddenly she said, "I know! Now I know! This is just half of the clam's shell. Find me another one and I'll show you."

Jean soon found another clam shell. Cathy put them together. "See, it's just like folding our hands together when we pray. The clam lives in between the two shells. See that place on the edges. That's probably a hinge so the two halves can open and shut. Don't you think that's the way it is?"

"I don't know," said Jean. "I never really thought about it."

The girls went on, but they did not find any other shell that Jean could name.

At last they turned back. Jean was glad. Cathy asked so many questions. She was very tired of saying "I don't know."

As they climbed slowly up the fifty wide steps to the top of the cliff, Jean said, "Cathy, I am sorry I couldn't answer your questions. I should not have said I know all about the ocean. I really don't know much after all.

"I think Mother and Daddy can give you all the information you need. And when they do, I am going to listen real hard to what they say."

–*Ruth K. Hobbs*

Seagull

The seagull curves his wings,
The seagull turns his eyes.
Get down into the water, fish!
(If you are wise).

    The seagull slants his wings,
    The seagull turns his head.
    Get down into the water, fish!
    (Or you'll be dead).

—Elizabeth Coatsworth

Do you know why the sea came up in
the holes this child had dug?

At the Seaside

When I was down beside the sea,
A wooden spade they gave to me
   To dig the sandy shore.

   My holes were empty like a cup.
   In every hole the sea came up,
      Till it could come no more.

—Robert Louis Stevenson

> *"Blessed is he that considereth the poor."*
>
> – Psalm 41:1

Quarrel at the Ritter Place

Part 1

"Daddy, you must help me think of something!" cried Randy the minute he opened the door of the woodworking shop.

"What are you talking about?" asked Daddy, looking up from the board he was sanding.

Randy took the push broom from its place on the wall. He began to sweep up the sawdust and shavings around Daddy's workbench. That was his first job after school. As he worked, he talked.

"We had a missionary at school today. He came from Haiti. He showed us Haiti on the map. He told us about the country and about the people. He told us how poor they are and what kind of houses they live in and what they eat and what they do for a living.

"Then he told about the children's home where they take care of children who have no fathers or mothers. We all felt so sorry for them.

"After he left, we talked about how we might help them. We decided the children's home would be our Thanksgiving **project** this year."

"What are you going to do?" asked Daddy.

"Well, we had a lot of ideas, but none of them were very good. I guess we don't know much about how those poor children live and what they would really need.

"So Miss Wine said it might be best to send money to the missionary. Then he could buy something he knows would make the poor children happy."

"Where are you going to get money?" Daddy asked next.

"That's why I need you to help me," said Randy. "Between now and Thanksgiving we all are going to make as much money as we can. On the first day after Thanksgiving vacation, we will bring the money we made and tell how we made it. Then Miss Wine will send it to the missionary.

"Our parents can't just give us money to bring. We children are supposed to make the money ourselves."

"I'll have to think about that," said Daddy. "There isn't a whole lot of time between now and Thanksgiving. And third graders are hardly big enough to go out and get jobs."

"I know," put in Randy. "That's what we told Miss Wine. She said our parents can help us all they want to. They just aren't supposed to give us money to bring. We have to help make the money."

"Do you have any ideas?" asked Daddy.

"Not really. I thought you could help me make something here in the shop. It would have to be something I could sell. But I don't know what it could be."

"Well, let's think about it for a day or so. We will come up with something," said Daddy.

Randy finished sweeping and went into the house. As he walked in, he heard his mother say, "Oh, here he is now. I'll ask him."

Mother turned from the phone and said, "Phil wonders if you can meet him at the Ritter place in about ten minutes."

"Sure," answered Randy, "if it is all right with you."

Mother turned back to the phone. "Yes, Phil. He can come for a while. He will be there in about ten minutes." Then she hung up.

"You and Phil should have been brothers instead of cousins," she said with a laugh. "You never get tired of being together, and you have never had a quarrel that I know of."

"Well, I don't have a brother, and his brother is a baby, so we need each other." Randy went out the door and up the back lane toward the woods.

The woods stood halfway between the two farms. The boys' fathers owned it. As long as Randy and Phil could remember, an old house had stood in a little open space in the trees. Their fathers had let a poor family live there without paying rent.

But that summer the house had burned down. The Ritters had to find another place to live.

Since then, the boys often played in the woods near what was left of the burned-down house. They often met there to talk.

Today when they both got there, the boys sat on the stone wall and talked about the Ritters.

"Do you think the Ritters were as poor as the people in Haiti?" asked Phil.

"Oh, no, not nearly as poor," said Randy. "The Ritters had a pig and a cow and hens. Most people in Haiti aren't that rich."

"But the pig died and the cow got sick and they couldn't milk her," answered Phil. "And a fox got their hens."

"No wonder. They shouldn't have let them run loose," said Randy. "They should have fixed up the old henhouse and kept them penned up."

"They likely didn't have enough money to fix up the henhouse or to buy chicken feed. That's why they let the hens run loose."

"Well, our dads let them live here free, and they had a garden. Mother said Mrs. Ritter had a good garden started. Most people in Haiti don't have a big garden like the Ritters did."

"I guess you are right. But look at that garden now. It is one big weed patch," said Phil. "But what I really want to talk about is our Thanksgiving project. Do you have any good ideas about how we could make some money?"

"Not really. I told Daddy about it a while ago. We want a project we can make in the shop."

"Where would you sell it?" asked Phil.

"I don't know. Maybe at the Jamesburg Market. I heard some of the girls talking about making cookies to sell there."

"I just wish it were spring," said Phil. "Then we could raise popcorn or watermelons or something like that to sell. But here it is fall already. It is going to be hard to think of something to do that will bring in any money."

Just then, far across the field they heard the *dong, dong* of a bell.

"That's for me," said Randy, hopping off the wall. "See you tomorrow. Think of something for us to do if you can."

After school the next day, Randy went to the shop. The first thing he said was, "Daddy, have you thought of something I can do to make money?"

"No, I haven't," said Daddy. "I did think of some things, but I don't know where you could sell them."

Randy took down the push broom and began to work. "I thought I could make birdhouses. But no one would buy birdhouses this time of the year.

"And I thought about bird feeders. But one of the other boys said his father was going to help him make bird feeders to sell at the Jamesburg Market. So I can't make bird feeders. That was before Miss Wine said we'd better not be telling each other what we planned to do.

"She said if one of us had a good idea, a lot of others might want to do the same thing, and that would not be fair.

"And she also said two of us might think of the same thing, but if we didn't know the other was doing it, that would be all right."

Daddy laughed. "Do you think you and Phil can keep from telling each other what you are doing?"

"Oh, sure," said Randy. "I just wish I knew of something to do."

"Maybe we need to ask the Lord to help us think of something," said Daddy.

"Yes, let's do that every day from now on. I want to get to work on whatever I'm going to do. Maybe God will give us some good ideas since we are making money for poor people."

So every day Mother and Daddy and Randy prayed

for a good idea. They prayed for something they could do to make money for the poor children in Haiti.

The week went by. The next week went by. Mother and Daddy and Randy had talked over many plans for making money. But none of them seemed like a very good idea.

On Friday, Randy came home from school almost in tears. "Mother, what are we going to do? All the other children are working on their projects but Phil and me."

"How do you know that?" asked Mother. "I thought you weren't to talk about your projects."

"Oh, they don't talk about it. But they smile and nod their heads at each other and roll their eyes around at Phil and me. That means they know what they are going to do. And they know Phil and I don't have anything yet."

"Let's not worry about it," said Mother. "We are asking God to help us. So I believe He will give us an idea in plenty of time before Thanksgiving."

"But we have prayed for two weeks. And Phil said they are praying too."

"How about making something that we could sell at Jamesburg Market?"

"Well, the girls were talking about selling cookies there. And one boy is making bird feeders," said Randy.

"That leaves a lot of things we could make," said

337

Mother. "Cakes and pies and bread and ice cream and candy."

"I couldn't help much with that kind of stuff, could I?"

"Oh, yes. I could give you plenty to do," said Mother.

On Saturday morning Phil called Randy on the phone. When Randy hung up, he said, "We have a plan, Mother. Phil wants me to meet him at the Ritter place right after lunch today. He is going to tell me everything they talked about at their house. I am going to tell him all we talked about doing. He thinks maybe we can get an idea from each other. But of course, we wouldn't tell if we got a good idea from the other one."

"That might work," said Mother.

After lunch, Randy headed for the woods. He was gone a long time. When he came into the house, he wore a big smile on his face.

"Mother," he called in an excited voice. "Now I know what we can do to make Thanksgiving money!"

"That's wonderful," said Mother. "So you did get an idea from Phil?"

"No. He didn't come. I waited and waited."

Then Mother said, "Now I remember that Aunt Betty told me they were going to the city this afternoon. Then they were going on to their grandmother's for the weekend. Maybe they had a late lunch and there wasn't time for Phil to come to the woods. It would have been nice if he had called and told you he couldn't come.

Then you wouldn't have gone up there for nothing."

"I don't care, Mother!" cried Randy. "It wasn't for nothing! While I was waiting, I walked around the old burned-down house. And guess what I found back in the Ritters' old weedy garden? Now I know what my Thanksgiving project can be!"

—Ruth K. Hobbs

"But grievous words stir up anger."

– Proverbs 15:1

Quarrel at the Ritter Place

Part 2

"I could never guess," said Mother. "What did you find in Ritters' old garden?"

"There's a pumpkin back there in the weeds. I think it would make a lot of pies. Couldn't we make pumpkin pies to sell at Jamesburg Market?"

"Indeed, we could," said Mother. "I've got a good recipe. Pumpkin pies should sell well just before Thanksgiving. See, the Lord answered our prayers in plenty of time."

"Yes, I thought of that," said Randy. "And I thanked Him and thanked Him on the way home."

"Now, let's do a little planning," said Mother. "The pumpkin is likely good and ripe this time of the year.

Do you think you can get your wagon back there and bring it home?"

"I'll get it home somehow," said Randy. "Leave that part up to me."

"All right. Next Saturday you can bring it home. We will cook it and make filling. Then we will freeze it. Monday afternoon before Thanksgiving we can make the pies. We can sell them on Tuesday and Wednesday."

"Oh, I am so happy!" cried Randy. "Now I can smile and nod my head like the others."

Then Randy stopped smiling. "Oh, Mother, what about Phil? Now he's the only one without a project."

"Let's not worry about that," said Mother. "The Lord can find him something to do too. Don't be surprised if he comes home from his grandmother's with a better idea than yours."

Sure enough, on Monday morning Phil met Randy at the door of the schoolhouse. He was nodding and had a big grin on his face.

Randy broke into a happy laugh and nodded too.

Randy could hardly wait till Saturday. He could hardly wait to get the pumpkin home and show it to Mother.

Pulling his wagon through the woods was no fun. It was harder yet to yank it through the weeds that **encircled** the Ritters' burned-down house. Little by little he jerked it along the wall and back to the garden.

Then he stopped dead still. He could not believe what he saw through the tall weeds. But he had to believe it, for there was Phil in the garden. He was going the other way pulling a wagon. In the wagon was the pumpkin—Randy's pumpkin.

Randy dropped the handle of his wagon. "Phil!" he yelled. He went tearing through the weeds until he got to his cousin.

"Where are you going with my pumpkin?"

Phil turned around. Then he just stood there. Amazement was written all over his face.

"*Your* pumpkin?" he said. "What do you mean? This is *my* pumpkin."

"It is not!" cried Randy hotly. "I found it last week. It's for my Thanksgiving project. Mother and I are going to make pies to sell at the market."

"Not with this pumpkin!" said Phil. "This is mine. I found it last Saturday. And it's for *my* Thanksgiving project. Mama and I are going to make pumpkin bread to sell at the market."

"No, you're not!" cried Randy. "I saw this pumpkin first. You weren't even back here last Saturday."

"I was so! I came when I said. I was here before lunch, but you didn't come. I waited and waited. And while I was waiting, I walked back here and found this pumpkin."

"You did *not* say come before lunch. You said come

after lunch. And that's when I came. But you didn't come. That's when I found the pumpkin," cried Randy.

"I know good and well I never said *after* lunch," cried Phil. "We were going to the city and to Grandmother's after lunch. I couldn't even have come after lunch.

"And I saw this pumpkin *before* lunch, so I saw it first. That makes it mine." Phil turned away, pulling the wagon.

Randy was too angry to say another word. But he wasn't going to let Phil walk off with his whole Thanksgiving project.

He made a dash for the wagon. He put his arms around the pumpkin and tried to lift it off. It was so heavy he could hardly manage it and too huge to encircle completely.

He got it part way up. Then Phil looked back. "You leave my pumpkin alone!" he cried, giving the wagon a quick jerk. The wagon went out from under the pumpkin.

The pumpkin slipped out of Randy's arms. It hit the ground with a **thud** and split wide open!

Now Phil was the one who was angry. "Look what you did!" he cried, almost in tears. "I'm going to tell Mama on you! You've ruined my project!"

"You mean *you* ruined *my* project, and I don't care!" shouted Randy. "It was your fault. You jerked the wagon. I'm going to tell Mother on you too."

Both boys stood looking at the split pumpkin. Then Phil said, "Well, I'm taking the biggest piece. You can have the rest for your old pies."

He picked up the biggest piece and put it on his wagon. Without looking back he started for home.

Slowly Randy went back to his wagon. He pulled it to where the split pumpkin lay in the weeds and started to pick up the pieces.

All the fun had gone out of the Thanksgiving project. Tears began to run down his face.

By the time Randy got the wagon out of the woods, his tears were gone. He began to think about what Mother might say. He wished now he had not gotten so angry with Phil. He knew now that Phil really had seen the pumpkin first.

"But that didn't make it his," Randy said to himself. "Daddy owns the Ritter place just as much as Phil's dad does."

By the time Randy got to the house he was cross

all over again. The minute he walked in, Mother knew something was wrong. "What happened?" she asked.

Randy began to talk fast. "It's Phil. He took my pumpkin. He would have taken the whole thing if it hadn't split apart. But it was his fault. He jerked the wagon. And now I don't know if there is enough for our pies or not! Phil took most of it."

"Randy!" cried Mother. "What in the world are you talking about? You'd better slow down and start at the beginning."

So Randy slowed down and started at the beginning.

When he finished, Mother said, "I must call Aunt Betty and get Phil's side of this story. I can't believe you and Phil quarreled over a pumpkin. You could have cut it in half."

Mother went to the kitchen to call Aunt Betty. They talked for a long time. Randy could not hear what Mother said, but he could hear her laughing. He couldn't see what was so funny.

At last she came out. But all she said was, "Let's go and look at your pumpkin."

When she saw the broken pieces, she laughed. "Why, Randy, there is plenty of pumpkin here. We couldn't have used the whole thing anyhow. Now wasn't it silly to fight over it?"

Randy said nothing. By now he could see how silly it had been. He had enough pumpkin for his Thanksgiving project. So did Phil. So what was the quarrel all about?

Then Mother said, "You and Phil will have to patch up your quarrel. Right now would be the easiest time. But first I want to ask you some questions.

"Who said the first angry words over this pumpkin?"

Randy thought a little. "I guess I did. But, Mother, he was taking my pumpkin."

"Did Phil know it was your pumpkin?"

"Well, no. I guess he didn't when he first took it."

"Who had seen the pumpkin first?"

"Phil did. But I didn't know he had."

"After you knew Phil had seen the pumpkin first, what did you do?"

Randy didn't answer. Every question Mother asked showed him the whole quarrel had been pretty much his own fault.

He wished he had not gotten angry. He wished he had not yelled at Phil. He wished he had not tried to take the pumpkin. Most of all, he wished he and Phil were not mad at each other. But what could he do about it now?

"Wouldn't you like to run over to Aunt Betty's and tell Phil you are sorry?" asked Mother.

"I guess so. But I don't think it was all my fault," said Randy.

"I know that," said Mother. "You don't need to take the blame for everything. Just tell him you are sorry for what you did."

"All right, I will."

As soon as Randy said that, he began to feel happy. He began to run up the back lane toward the woods. When he got there he had to slow down and catch his breath.

He walked through the woods thinking about what he would say to Phil. He was almost at the Ritter place when he looked up.

And there, coming toward him was Phil.

–Ruth K. Hobbs

Do you think it is possible for someone to be wrong and right at the same time?

The Quarrel

I quarreled with my brother,
I don't know what about,
One thing led to another
And somehow we fell out.
The start of it was slight,
The end of it was strong,
He said he was right,
I knew he was wrong!

We hated one another.
The afternoon turned black.
Then suddenly my brother
Thumped me on the back,
And said, "Oh, come along!
We can't go on all night—
I was in the wrong."
So he was in the right.

—*Eleanor Farjeon*

> *"The light shall shine upon the ways."*
> – Job 22:28

Dora Makes a Way

Part 1

Years ago a little girl named Dora lived with her father in a lighthouse on a rocky island. Her father was the lightkeeper there. He took care of the big lamp at the top of the lighthouse. Every day he shined the glass around the lamp. He filled the lamp with oil and trimmed the wick carefully. Every night he lit the lamp.

Far out in the ocean, the sailors could see the light flashing. Then they could avoid the rocky island. Ships coming into the **harbor** on the mainland could also see the light. It told them exactly where they were and helped them avoid the rocky island.

If fog rolled in and hid the light, the keeper rang the big fog bell that hung outside the lighthouse. Sailors could hear the bell even though they could not see the light. The lightkeeper kept ringing the bell until the fog cleared away.

Dora had no mother. She could not go to school because the schoolhouse was on the mainland. Her father was her teacher. All the stores and shops were on the mainland too.

But Dora was happy. She was not lonely with her father. She kept the lighthouse clean. She cooked the meals and **recited** her lessons to her father every day.

In the evening when it was time to light the big lamp, Dora liked to climb the winding stairs with Father. Sometimes he held her up and let her put the match to the wick to light the lamp.

But Dora never rang the fog bell. Her father said that pulling the bell rope was a man's work because the bell and the rope were so heavy.

Dora knew how important the light and the fog bell were. She knew that sailors could wreck their ships and lose their lives if they could not see the light or hear the fog bell.

Every afternoon the boat from Boston passed the island on its way to the harbor on the mainland. Dora liked to wave to the sailors. Sometimes the sailors waved to her. Dora often wished she could ride on the boat to Boston and back again. Father had said there were wonderful things to see in Boston, but he didn't suppose they would ever get to go there.

One day at noon, Father said, "Dora, I must go to the mainland. We need groceries and some other things. I'll try to be back in two or three hours. I don't like to leave you alone, but God will be with you. He will help you do anything that needs to be done. Try to have supper ready when I return."

"All right," said Dora.

Father went off in his little rowboat. Dora watched as long as she could see him. Then she went to work. She washed the dishes and put them away. She swept the floor and dusted the chairs. She wiped the table and shook the rugs. That ended her housework.

Dora ran down the rocky path to the shore. There she began to hunt for shells. After a long time she felt a drop of rain. She had not paid any attention to the sky while she hunted shells. Now she saw that dark clouds filled the sky. A cold wind began to blow.

Dora gathered up her shells and ran for the lighthouse. She got there just as it began to rain hard. She stood by the window and looked toward the mainland, hoping to see her father's rowboat coming. But the rain fell faster and faster until it **blotted out** the mainland.

Then she thought of supper. "I will get supper ready. That will help pass the time until Father comes," she said to herself.

She spread the cloth and set the table. She made a fire in the stove and lit the little table lamp. She set it in the window for her father to see. Soon everything was bright and warm and cozy. But her father did not come.

Dora began making supper. All the while rain beat against the windows. She could hear the wind screaming around the lighthouse. She said to herself, "The rain has blotted out the mainland so I can't see it. It will also have blotted out the island and lighthouse so Father can't see it." And when she heard the thunder of the waves on the rocks, she knew her father would not be able to row across from the mainland in his small boat.

Suddenly she noticed that, although it was not yet night, the driving rain made it so dark that sailors would not be able to see the lighthouse or the island through the rain. Then she thought about the boat from Boston. It was almost time for it to be coming into the harbor. There must be a light to warn the sailors away from the rocks.

"The big lamp must be lit," Dora said to herself. "And I am the only one to do it!"

–adapted

> *"Seek the Lord and his strength."*
>
> – 1 Chronicles 16:11

Dora Makes a Way

Part 2

Dora took the kitchen lamp and some matches. She started up the long stairway that curved round and round until she reached the lamp room at the top of the lighthouse. She set the lamp down. Her first task was to turn up the wick of the big lamp and trim it. Then she saw that she was too short.

"I must have something to stand on," she said.

Down the long stairway she ran for her little stool. Back up the long curved stairs she came, only to discover that she still could not reach the lamp.

"I'll get a wooden box," she said. Down the stairs she went, then up again. With the stool on the box, at last she could reach the big lamp.

Dora turned up the wick and trimmed off the black burned part as she had seen Father do. She struck a match and touched it to the wick. How glad she was to see the flame blaze high. She closed the glass. The shade began to go round and round, making the light go *flash, flash, flash.*

How glad I am that I could light the lamp. Now the sailors on the Boston boat can find their way safely into the harbor, she thought happily. She picked up the wooden box and her stool and made her way down the stairs for the third time.

Dora went to the door and looked out. The storm seemed to have passed on as suddenly as it had come up. The wind had died and it was not raining much. But what she saw filled her heart with fear. A heavy fog was rolling in from the ocean. It blotted out the harbor. It blotted out the land and the rocks. She looked up at the light, and her heart leaped wildly. She could see only a dim *flash, flash, flash* from where she stood. The sailors on the Boston boat would not be able to see it at all from the sea. How could they avoid the island?

"The fog bell!" she said to herself. "I must ring the fog bell!" But how could she? Father said that was a man's work. It was too hard a **task** for a girl. Yet she was the only one to do it.

"God will help you do anything that needs to be done." Her father's parting words came to Dora's mind.

She must ring the fog bell. God would help her.

The fog bell hung on the outside of the lighthouse. The rope entered in through a hole and hung at the bottom of the stairs. Dora took hold of the rope and pulled. Nothing happened. She tried again, but the bell did not ring. "Dear God, help me know what to do," she prayed.

She said to herself, "Maybe if I go partway up the stairs and take hold of the rope, it will ring when I walk down the steps."

Her idea was a good one. She went up a few steps and took hold of the rope as far up as she could. Holding it tightly she walked down the steps. Far above, she heard the bell clang. She walked up the steps again. Again the bell clanged.

Up and down, up and down she went again and again. Before long, Dora began to feel very tired. The rope hurt her hands, and her arms felt as though they would drop right off. But she could not stop. She must warn the Boston boat about the rocks.

"God, help me keep the bell ringing," she prayed. On and on and on and on. *Dong, dong, dong, dong.*

At last the fog rolled away and daylight came. Dora's father rowed to the island as fast as he could. Up the rocks to the lighthouse he ran. There he found his little girl. She lay fast asleep on the stairs with the bell rope still in her hand. And the great light was still burning, *flash, flash, flash.*

A number of days later Dora and her father crossed to the mainland. There they happened to meet a sailor from the Boston boat who knew them. As they talked about the storm, the sailor said, "It's a good thing you started to ring that fog bell when you did, or we might not be here now. We were pretty close in to the island when you began to ring the bell."

"Oh, but I didn't ring the bell," said Dora's father. "That was my little girl." Then he explained what had happened.

"And I didn't ring it all by myself," said Dora. "I wasn't nearly strong enough. God helped me."

"I guess you saved my life and the lives of a good many others that night," said the sailor. "How can I say thank you? Perhaps I can fix things so that you and your father can ride to Boston with us on our next trip. Would you enjoy that?"

Dora was almost too surprised and happy to speak. Her voice would not come out right. But she did whisper, "Oh, yes. I would enjoy that."

You can be sure that Dora was on the boat the next time it went to Boston.

–adapted

In many places there are foghorns instead of fog bells. This poem helps you "hear" how foghorns sound—even if you never have heard one.

The Foghorn

Foggy, foggy over the water,
Foggy, foggy over the bay,
Foggy, so foggy the boats are like shadows
And how can they find their way?

Far away and over the water
Hear the voice of the foghorn say,
"Whoo-oo-oo, I'm guiding you,
Boats that are out on the bay."

Foggy, foggy over the water,
Foggy, foggy over the bay,
And through the fog the boats go slowly
While the foghorn tells them the way.

—Edith H. Newlin

A lighthouse keeper or a sailor might not enjoy misty,
foggy fall weather as much as the writer of this poem did.

The Mist and All

I like the fall,
The mist and all.
I like the night owl's
Lonely call—
And wailing sound
Of wind around.

I like the gray
November day,
And bare dead boughs
That coldly sway
Against my pane.
I like the rain.

I like to sit
And laugh at it—
And tend
My cozy fire a bit.
I like the fall—
The mist and all.

–Dixie Willson

> *"As the LORD liveth, and as thy soul liveth,*
> *I will not leave thee."*
>
> – 2 Kings 2:2

I Won't Leave You

1. And it came to pass, when the LORD would take up Elijah into heaven by a whirlwind, that Elijah went with Elisha from Gilgal.

2. And Elijah said unto Elisha, Tarry here, I pray thee; for the LORD hath sent me to Bethel. And Elisha said unto him, As the LORD liveth, and as thy soul liveth, I will not leave thee. So they went down to Bethel.

3. And the sons of the prophets that were at Bethel came forth to Elisha, and said unto him, Knowest thou that the LORD will take away thy master from thy head to day? And he said, Yea, I know it; hold ye your peace.

4. And Elijah said unto him, Elisha, tarry here, I pray thee; for the LORD hath sent me to Jericho. And he said, As the LORD liveth, and as thy soul liveth, I will not leave thee. So they came to Jericho.

5. And the sons of the prophets that were at Jericho came to Elisha, and said unto him, Knowest thou that the LORD will take away thy master from thy head to day? And he answered, Yea, I know it; hold ye your peace.

6. And Elijah said unto him, Tarry, I pray thee, here; for the LORD hath sent me to Jordan. And he said, As the LORD liveth, and as thy soul liveth, I will not leave thee. And they two went on.

7. And fifty men of the sons of the prophets went, and stood to view afar off: and they two stood by Jordan.

8. And Elijah took his mantle, and wrapped it together, and smote the waters, and they were divided hither and thither, so that they two went over on dry ground.

9. And it came to pass, when they were gone over, that Elijah said unto Elisha, Ask what I shall do for thee, before I be taken away from thee. And Elisha said, I pray thee, let a double **portion** of thy spirit be upon me.

10. And he said, Thou hast asked a hard thing: nevertheless, if thou see me when I am taken from thee, it shall be so unto thee; but if not, it shall not be so.

11. And it came to pass, as they still went on, and talked, that, behold, there appeared a chariot of fire, and horses of fire, and parted them both asunder; and Elijah went up by a whirlwind into heaven.

12. And Elisha saw it, and he cried, My father, my father, the chariot of Israel, and the horsemen thereof. And he saw him no more.

–2 Kings 2:1-12

Glossary

Every word that is in boldfaced type in *Doors to Discovery* is in this glossary. With each word you will find the dictionary pronunciation and a definition. The definition given is for the way the word is used in the story in this book. Many of these words have other definitions. The sample sentence in italics shows how to use the word correctly. The page number following the sentence indicates where the word is found in the reader.

accomplish (ə käm′ plish): to bring about by trying. *Dorothy worked hard to accomplish all the jobs Mom asked her to do.* 209

accused (ə kyüzd′): blamed for doing wrong. *Joseph accused his brothers of being spies.* 220

admitted (əd mi′ təd): confessed or agreed that something is true. *Norma admitted she had hidden the book.* 36

aggravate (a′ grə vāt): to bother or make angry. *Valerie tried not to let Dale's teasing aggravate her.* 28

amend (ə mend′): to improve or change for the better. *The missionary wanted to amend the poor living conditions of the people.* 276

ascending (ə sen′ diŋ): going upward from a lower place. *We watched the balloon ascending until it was only a tiny red speck against the blue sky.* 134

assignments (ə sīn′ mənts): lessons that are given to be completed. *Miss Layne gave us three short assignments.* 22

assured (ə shùrd′): told or promised in a sure way. *When James asked if the lamb was really his, Daddy assured him it was.* 168

astonished (ə stä′ nisht): filled with great surprise. *Grandma was astonished when she found a beautiful rose lying on the table.* 33

attached (ə tacht′): fastened. *Mr. Hobbs attached the sign to the window.* 181

avoid (ə vòid′): to stay away from. *The cat tried to avoid the mud puddles.* 57

awl (òl): a pointed tool used to punch holes in wood or leather. *The shoemaker used an awl as he sewed the pieces of the shoe together.* 227

barge (bärj): a large, flat-bottomed boat used for carrying goods on rivers or canals. *A coal barge holds hundreds of tons of coal.* 107

bawled (bòld): cried loudly. *The calf bawled when it ran into the electric fence.* 239

bear (ber) : 1. to be able to stand something. *Isaac couldn't bear seeing the rabbit suffer.* 84
2. to hold and carry. *Jaden will bear the stack of books to the library.* 98

bewildered (bi wil′ dərd) : puzzled or confused. *The loud honking of car horns bewildered the lost dog.* 195

billowed (bi′ lōd) : rose or swelled. *The boat raced through the water as the sails billowed in the wind.* 223

blessing (bles′ iŋ) : something that brings joy or happiness. *Zachary thanked God for the blessing of rain.* 246

blizzard (bli′ zərd) : a long, hard snowstorm. *Dad was glad there was plenty of food in the house when the blizzard hit.* 182

blotted out (blä′ təd aùt) : wiped out or made hard to see. *The clouds blotted out the moon before the boys got their tent set up.* 352

broad (bròd) : large and wide. *The broad leaves of the plant provided shade for the panting dog.* 117

bustle (bə′ səl) : busy activity. *What noise and bustle filled the classroom on the last day of school!* 118

carriage (ker′ ij) : a vehicle with wheels used for carrying people, usually pulled by horses. *Four black horses pulled the carriage down the street.* 66

Pronunciation Key

/a/ bat; /ā/ acorn; /är/ star; /e/ pet; /ē/ eagle; /er/ bear; /ər/ her; /i/ bit; /ī/ ivy; /ir/ deer; /ä/ top; /ō/ go; /ò/ lost; /òi/ coin; /aù/ out; /òr/ corn; /ə/ but; /ü/ boot; /yü/ use; /ú/ foot; /th/ thick; /<u>th</u>/ this; /ŋ/ bang; /zh/ measure

ceased (sēst): stopped. *When Jesus spoke, the wind ceased.* 65

cells (selz): the hollow, waxy spaces in a honeycomb that bees make to store honey and eggs. *The bees filled the cells with honey.* 303

charred (chärd): made black by burning. *Ralph ate the charred hot dog.* 249

churned (chərnd): stirred cream in a churn to make butter. *Merle spread the freshly churned butter on a slice of warm bread.* 45

cloak (klōk): a loose garment, often without sleeves, that is worn like a coat. *Betsy tore her cloak when she climbed over the fence.* 40

clustered (kləs' tərd): gathered in a group. *The chicks clustered around the water dish.* 167

comforters (kəm' fər tərz): thick, warm covers for a bed. *The girls stayed cozy under the comforters.* 287

companion (kəm pan' yən): a person who goes with another. *When Mr. Rucker visited Mexico, he chose Pedro to be his traveling companion.* 57

conference (kän' fə rəns): a meeting to talk about important matters. *All the teachers went to the conference.* 170

conquers (käŋ′ kərz) : takes control over. *The Bible says that the person who conquers his temper is better than the person who conquers a city.* 35

construct (kən strəkt′) : to make or build. *The boys decided to construct a tree house out of the old boards.* 247

consumed (kən sümd′) : ate or used up; destroyed. *The fire consumed the old barn.* 165

contrary (kän′ trer ē) : against; not helpful. *The wind was contrary to the little sailboat.* 65

coward (kaủ′ ərd) : a person without courage or who is easily frightened. *Randy was too much of a coward to admit he had broken the window.* 81

critical (kri′ ti kəl) : quick to find fault or to blame. *Mary Beth is not a critical person; she always speaks kindly of others.* 314

cunning (kə′ niŋ) : quick in thinking and reasoning; clever. *Ronald gave a cunning answer to Regina's riddle.* 27

cutter (kə′ tər) : a small ship used by the government. *The Coast Guard cutter picked up the people from the shipwreck.* 296

departed (dē pär′ təd) : left; went away. *The bear departed after eating all the honey.* 64

deserted (di zər′ təd): left empty. *The boys wanted to explore the deserted barn.* 285

discouragement (dis kər′ ij mənt): a feeling of little hope or courage. *"When will we be finished peeling potatoes?" asked Lillian in discouragement.* 160

dismiss (dis mis′): to allow to leave. *Papa will dismiss us from the table after we have sung a song.* 265

downcast (daủn′ kast): looking down; very sad. *With downcast eyes, Kevin told us that he had lost the keys to the truck.* 88

dread (dred): to feel fear or worry about something that will happen. *God helped Josie not to dread going to a new school.* 28

dreadful (dred′ fəl): very bad or scary. *Linda had a dreadful scare when Jeremy threw the dead mouse at her.* 34

dress (dres): to prepare an animal or bird for cooking. *Mother said, "I will help you pick peas after I dress these two chickens."* 162

duty (dü′ tē): something one ought to do. *It was Richard's duty to watch his little brother while he played outside.* 213

earnestly (ər′ nəst lē): very seriously; not playfully. *Lawrence earnestly asked Nancy to help him finish his chores.* 152

eased (ēzd): moved carefully. *Grandpa eased his tired body into bed.* 108

employer (im ploi′ ər): the person for whom someone works for pay. *Wendel's employer gave him a day off to attend a wedding.* 61

encircled (en sər′ kəld): made a circle around something. *Pine trees encircled Uncle Rob's farm.* 341

errand (er′ ənd): a short trip taken to do a job for someone. *Herman asked Bradley to run an errand for him.* 62

eventually (i ven′ shwə lē): sometime later; in the end. *A toddler who keeps trying will eventually learn how to walk.* 269

exhausted (ig zȯs′ təd): 1. very tired and worn out. *Everyone was exhausted after climbing to the top of the mountain.* 169
2. used up. *The nurses exhausted the supply of bandages.* 182

expensive (ik spen′ siv): costing a lot of money. *Few people could buy the expensive books.* 230

experimenting (ik sper′ ə men tiŋ): testing or trying out something to see if it works. *Derrick is experimenting with ways to make ink from plants.* 231

Pronunciation Key
/a/ **bat**; /ā/ **acorn**; /är/ **star**; /e/ **pet**; /ē/ **eagle**; /er/ **bear**; /ər/ **her**; /i/ **bit**; /ī/ **ivy**; /ir/ **deer**; /ä/ **top**; /ō/ **go**; /ȯ/ **lost**; /ȯi/ **coin**; /au̇/ **out**; /ȯr/ **corn**; /ə/ **but**; /ü/ **boot**; /yü/ **use**; /u̇/ **foot**; /th/ **thick**; /<u>th</u>/ **this**; /ŋ/ **bang**; /zh/ **measure**

extremely (ik strēm′ lē) : very much. *Julie is extremely happy to have a baby sister.* 223

fade (fād) : to become pale or less bright. *The stars began to fade as daylight came.* 10

faithful (fāth′ fəl) : staying true to someone or something. *Jesus said people who are faithful in small things will also be faithful in bigger things.* 214

ferry (fer′ ē) : a boat that carries people and things across a body of water. *The ferry took the people and their cars to the island.* 292

fervently (fər′ vənt lē) : with strong feeling. *The children fervently hoped that it would snow all night.* 168

fired (fīrd) : dismissed from a job. *The boss fired Donna because she did her work carelessly.* 219

fling (fliŋ) : a hard or careless throw. *Andrew gave his coat a fling onto the couch.* 76

foreign (fȯr′ ən) : someone or something from a different country. *Our foreign neighbor cannot speak English.* 161

forenoon (fȯr′ nün) : morning. *Edward went to school only in the forenoon.* 39

fortress (fȯr′ trəs) : a place built with strong walls to keep out enemies. *Our team built a fortress of snow before the big snowball battle.* 197

furiously (fyŭr′ ē əs lē): in an angry way. *The farmers furiously chased the fox that had stolen their chickens.* 224

furrow (fər′ ō): a long, narrow ditch in the soil made by a plow. *The robins hopped along in the furrow, looking for worms.* 216

gaily (gā′ lē): in a bright, cheerful way. *The gaily decorated room was the perfect place for a party.* 115

gauge (gāj): an instrument that measures things such as gasoline or air pressure. *Father got the tire gauge and checked all the tires.* 297

glimpses (glimp′ səz): short, quick looks. *The hunter caught a few glimpses of his dogs chasing the bear.* 196

glossy (glä′ sē): smooth and shiny. *The little boy carefully turned the glossy pages of the new book.* 119

goods (gŭdz): things to buy and sell. *Mrs. Eavey took her goods to the market to sell.* 108

grazed (grāzd): fed on grass or other plants. *Heather watched the goats as they grazed in the pasture.* 212

gushed (gəsht): shot out with force. *Water gushed from the broken pipe.* 163

Pronunciation Key

/a/ **ba**t; /ā/ **a**corn; /är/ **star**; /e/ **pe**t; /ē/ **eagle**; /er/ **bear**; /ər/ **her**; /i/ **bi**t; /ī/ **ivy**; /ir/ **deer**; /ä/ **top**; /ō/ **go**; /ò/ **lost**; /òi/ **coin**; /aů/ **out**; /òr/ **corn**; /ə/ **but**; /ü/ **boot**; /yü/ **use**; /ů/ **foot**; /th/ **thick**; /<u>th</u>/ **this**; /ŋ/ **bang**; /zh/ **measure**

harbor (här′ bər): the part of an ocean near land where the water is deep enough for ships to find shelter. *The fishing boat made it into the harbor just ahead of the storm.* 350

hazy (hā′ zē): dim or cloudy. *The smoke from the forest fires made the air hazy.* 182

hearth (härth): the brick or stone floor in front of a fireplace. *We knelt on the hearth to toast marshmallows.* 49

hedge (hej): a fence made of shrubs or low trees. *We planted a hedge around our property.* 70

hitched (hicht): fastened with a hook or knot. *Howard hitched the horses to the wagon.* 127

hobbled (hä′ bəld): walked with a limp. *Grace hobbled into the living room and sat down on the recliner.* 70

hogan (hō′ gän): an Indian house built of logs and mud. *The morning sun shone in through the hogan door.* 133

igloos (i′ glüz): Eskimo houses made of blocks of snow. *The hunters built igloos for themselves.* 174

ignorant (ig′ nə rənt): not having much knowledge. *Because Stanley did not care about learning, he grew up to be an ignorant man.* 22

illegal (i lē′ gəl): against the law. *It is illegal to throw trash out of a car window.* 277

injury (inj′ rē): hurt or damage. *The injury to Christine's fingers happened when she got them pinched in the door.* 88

innocent (i′ nə sənt): not guilty. *Fred thought Lucy had played the trick, but she was innocent.* 217

inquired (in kwīrd′): asked. *Mr. Franklin inquired if we had eggs to sell.* 123

inspected (in spek′ təd): looked at very carefully. *The teacher inspected Henry's paper for misspelled words.* 59

instructed (in strək′ təd): told what to do. *Mr. Risser instructed the class to start the game without him.* 240

ivory (ī′ və rē): the hard creamy-white material that forms the tusks of animals such as the walrus and elephant. *Eskimos carve beautiful things from the ivory of the walrus.* 175

jailer (jā′ lər): the person in charge of a jail. *The jailer made sure the prisoner would not escape.* 191

keen (kēn): deep, strong, or sharp. *Conner took a keen interest in the softball game.* 56

lagging (la′ giŋ): falling behind. *The youngest students were soon lagging behind.* 55

Pronunciation Key
/a/ bat; /ā/ acorn; /är/ star; /e/ pet; /ē/ eagle; /er/ bear; /ər/ her; /i/ bit; /ī/ ivy; /ir/ deer; /ä/ top; /ō/ go; /ò/ lost; /òi/ coin; /aủ/ out; /òr/ corn; /ə/ but; /ü/ boot; /yü/ use; /ủ/ foot; /th/ thick; /th/ this; /ŋ/ bang; /zh/ measure

locomotive (lō kə mō′ tiv): an engine that pulls railroad cars. *The bright headlights of the locomotive shone on the tracks.* 292

lopsided (läp′ sī dəd): not evenly shaped. *Heidi was disappointed with the lopsided cake.* 312

lull (ləl): a period of quiet in the middle of noise or a storm. *When a stranger entered the room, there was a lull in the conversation.* 195

lush (ləsh): full of thick, healthy growth. *Lush green plants grow in the rain forest.* 121

meal (mēl): crushed grain. *Aunt Amelia used the last of the meal to make fried mush.* 182

menu (men′ yü): a list of foods that will be served. *Mrs. Lambert looked at the menu and then ordered fried chicken, mashed potatoes, and a roll.* 92

midst (midst): middle. *The boat was in the midst of the lake.* 64

mischief (mis′ chəf): small bothersome deeds done in a playful way. *Mother tied up the puppy to keep him from getting into mischief.* 86

misdeeds (mis dēdz′): wrong things that are done. *William confessed his misdeeds to his parents.* 81

moccasins (mä′ kə sənz): soft leather shoes without heels. *Little Fox's moccasins made no sound in the wet leaves.* 253

mounds (maúndz) : rounded heaps. *Ricky heaped two mounds of mashed potatoes onto his plate.* 109

mufflers (mə′ flərz) : scarves worn around the neck for warmth. *Roger and Oscar put on their boots, coats, and mufflers, and then ran out to play in the snow.* 294

nasty (nas′ tē) : not nice; disgusting. *Caitlin found a nasty skunk skeleton in the basement.* 35

oaken (ō′ kən) : made from the wood of an oak tree. *The old chairs were oaken, but the new chairs were pine.* 48

ointment (óint′ mənt) : a soothing and healing cream for the skin. *The ointment felt so good on the burned skin.* 278

orchard (òr′ chərd) : a piece of land on which fruit trees are grown. *Mom and Eugene went to the orchard to pick peaches.* 238

ownership (ō′ nər ship) : the state of being an owner. *Norman was happy to claim ownership of the new roller skates.* 282

pester (pes′ tər) : to bother or disturb. *Most people do not enjoy having someone pester them.* 27

plantation (plan tā′ shən) : a large farm on which the workers live and help grow a main crop. *When the cotton was ripe, the plantation looked as if snow had fallen on it.* 116

Pronunciation Key
/a/ bat; /ā/ acorn; /är/ star; /e/ pet; /ē/ eagle; /er/ bear; /ər/ her; /i/ bit; /ī/ ivy; /ir/ deer; /ä/ top; /ō/ go; /ò/ lost;
/ói/ coin; /aú/ out; /òr/ corn; /ə/ but; /ü/ boot; /yü/ use; /ù/ foot; /th/ thick; /<u>th</u>/ this; /ŋ/ bang; /zh/ measure

pleasure (ple′ zhər): happiness and enjoyment. *The baker said it was his pleasure to serve us fresh cinnamon rolls.* 43

pod (päd): a group of sea animals, such as whales. *The pod of whales swam about the ocean, looking for a place to rest and eat.* 270

pondered (pän′ dərd): thought about carefully. *Edwin pondered the question for a few minutes before he answered it.* 313

portion (pȯr′ shən): a part of something. *Everyone got a portion of the pie.* 361

possessions (pə ze′ shənz): the things a person owns. *The family loaded all their possessions onto the oxcart.* 153

prod (präd): to poke with a stick. *Dave used the hoe handle to prod the pig into the barn.* 103

prop (präp): an object that holds something up. *Abigail used the chair as a prop for her aching leg.* 280

punctured (pəŋk′ chərd): pierced with a sharp object. *Nails on the driveway punctured one of the truck's tires.* 227

pupils (pyü′ pəlz): students. *The pupils decided to see how many books they could read.* 177

project (prä′ jekt): something that is planned and carried out for a special reason. *For a project this summer, Tyler plans to grow and sell tomatoes.* 332

provide (prə vīd′): to make available what is needed. *We know that God will provide for us.* 152

quavered (kwā′ vərd): shook or trembled. *Judith's voice quavered with fear as she called Lassie's name again and again.* 68

rebelling (ri be′ liŋ): fighting or working against leaders. *The king punished the servants who were rebelling against him.* 196

recited (ri sī′ təd): repeated something aloud. *Justin recited his math facts.* 350

refuge (re′ fyüj): a shelter from danger. *The deer looked for a refuge from the hounds.* 197

resist (ri zist′): to refuse to give in to something. *Caleb said he would resist the temptation to whisper during the church service.* 171

rinsed (rinst): removed dirt by lightly washing. *Gary rinsed the garbage pail at the garden pump.* 61

salute (sə lüt′): to greet a person. *The friendly old gentleman likes to salute everyone he passes on the sidewalk.* 203

scampered (skam′ pərd): ran around in a lively and playful way. *The goats scampered through the soybean field.* 16

Pronunciation Key

/a/ bat; /ā/ acorn; /är/ star; /e/ pet; /ē/ eagle; /er/ bear; /ər/ her; /i/ bit; /ī/ ivy; /ir/ deer; /ä/ top; /ō/ go; /ȯ/ lost; /ȯi/ coin; /au̇/ out; /ȯr/ corn; /ə/ but; /ü/ boot; /yü/ use; /u̇/ foot; /th/ thick; /t͟h/ this; /ŋ/ bang; /zh/ measure

scorn (skȯrn): a feeling that someone is not worthy of being respected. *Mom reproved Mike for showing scorn toward his brother.* 33

seized (sēzd): grabbed. *Marcus seized the hoe and began to chop weeds.* 86

settlers (set' lərz): people who move to a new area to live. *The settlers cut down trees to build cabins.* 182

shawl (shȯl): a large piece of cloth worn over the shoulders or head. *The old woman pulled her shawl tightly around her shoulders.* 70

shingles (shiŋ' gəlz): thin, flat pieces of building material used to cover a roof. *Marvin chose gray shingles for the new roof.* 286

shouldered (shōl' dərd): placed on the shoulder. *As he left the house, Michael shouldered his gun.* 45

shriek (shrēk): a loud, sharp cry. *Mom heard Beth shriek when the spider ran across the floor.* 146

shuffled (shə' fəld): mixed; arranged in a different order. *Holly shuffled the papers.* 68

skillfully (skil' fə lē): having the ability to do something well. *Grandma skillfully patted the bread dough into loaves.* 129

sleek (slēk): smooth and shiny. *The little Mexican girl had sleek black hair.* 271

sluggard (slə′ gərd): a lazy person. *A sluggard does not put much effort into his work.* 53

slung (sləŋ): threw with a sweeping motion. *Philip slung his backpack onto his bed.* 158

snaring (sner′ iŋ): catching small birds or animals by a kind of loop trap. *Thomas helped bring food to his family by snaring rabbits.* 253

snitched (snicht): stole something small in a sneaky way. *Mollie was sorry she had snitched the candy.* 265

snoopy (snü′ pē): trying to find out things that are none of your business. *It is snoopy to look into the teacher's desk without permission.* 305

soberly (sō′ bər lē): with a serious expression. *Janet soberly rewrote her sloppy penmanship lesson.* 26

sod (säd): the top layer of soil with the grass and its roots. *The farmer plowed the sod so he could plant corn.* 174

sodden (sä′ dən): heavy with water. *After the sudden thunderstorm, the towels on the clothesline were sodden.* 287

soggy (sä′ gē): very wet; soaked with a liquid. *Tyler gave the soggy bread to his kitten.* 111

soles (sōlz): the bottom part of the feet. *The soles of Paul's feet were covered with blisters.* 98

Pronunciation Key

/a/ bat; /ā/ acorn; /är/ star; /e/ pet; /ē/ eagle; /er/ bear; /ər/ her; /i/ bit; /ī/ ivy; /ir/ deer; /ä/ top; /ō/ go; /ȯ/ lost; /ȯi/ coin; /au̇/ out; /ȯr/ corn; /ə/ but; /ü/ boot; /yü/ use; /u̇/ foot; /th/ thick; /<u>th</u>/ this; /ŋ/ bang; /zh/ measure

soot (sút): the black powder that is made when things are burned. *Mom wanted the soot cleaned out of the chimney.* 288

sorrowful (sär′ ō fəl): feeling sad or troubled. *In a sorrowful voice, Kervin told Mr. Ellis he had broken the window.* 264

spattered (spa′ tərd): splashed with small drops. *When Kelly turned the mixer on high, chocolate batter spattered all over the counter.* 240

speechless (spēch′ ləs): not able to speak. *Cindy was speechless when Leah showed her the hidden door in the wall.* 225

spied (spīd): saw; spotted. *Chester spied Ruth's glove lying beside the path.* 41

splint (splint): something stiff that is tightly bound to a broken bone to keep it from moving. *The boys used a sawed-off broom handle as a splint for Patrick's broken arm.* 298

spokes (spōks): bars that connect a wheel's rim to its center part. *Arthur broke several spokes in his bicycle wheel when he had his wreck.* 87

spout (spaút): the tube or lip of a container from which liquid is poured. *When the water in the teakettle began to boil, steam rose out of the spout.* 207

sprouts (spraüts): the first shoots of plants as they begin to grow. *The alfalfa sprouts tasted delicious in the salad.* 105

sputtered (spə′ tərd): talked in a fast, confused way. *"I didn't know it would break," sputtered Ellen.* 219

stern (stərn): not gentle; harsh. *In a stern voice, the neighbor ordered Jeb to keep his dog at home.* 190

stilts (stilts): poles that hold something above the ground or water. *The house beside the river was built on stilts to keep the floodwaters out.* 100

stumped (stəmpt): puzzled; not able to figure out something. *The math question stumped even the teacher.* 94

stunned (stənd): unable to think or feel because of being hit hard. *A bump on the head stunned Elaine for a few minutes.* 272

suffer (sə′ fər): to feel pain or discomfort. *Gene freed the fox from the trap because he could not stand to see it suffer.* 25

surmising (sər mī′ ziŋ): forming an opinion without knowing the facts. *The children were surmising that Mom had planned a surprise.* 314

Pronunciation Key

/a/ **bat**; /ā/ **acorn**; /är/ **star**; /e/ **pet**; /ē/ **eagle**; /er/ **bear**; /ər/ **her**; /i/ **bit**; /ī/ **ivy**; /ir/ **deer**; /ä/ **top**; /ō/ **go**; /ò/ **lost**; /òi/ **coin**; /aù/ **out**; /òr/ **corn**; /ə/ **but**; /ü/ **boot**; /yü/ **use**; /ù/ **foot**; /th/ **thick**; /th/ **this**; /ŋ/ **bang**; /zh/ **measure**

synagogue (si′ nə gäg): a building where Jews meet
to worship. *Jesus often went to the synagogue to
teach.* 31

task (task): a job. *Dad gave Christopher the task of
cleaning out the garage.* 354

tender (ten′ dər): easy to break, cut, or chew. *Sue baked
the roast beef all night so that it would be tender.* 279

terror (ter′ ər): a feeling of great fear. *Terror filled the ewe
as she saw the eagle swoop toward her lamb.* 19

thatched (thacht): roofed with a plant material, such as
straw. *The thatched roof kept the little house warm and
dry.* 245

thrill (thril): a strong feeling that shoots through the body.
Louise felt a thrill of fear when she saw the lion. 129

thud (thəd): a dull sound. *The watermelon hit the floor
with a thud.* 343

tidal wave (tī′ dəl wāv): a high wave of the ocean that
can cause much damage; also called *tsunami. An
earthquake or volcano can cause a tidal wave.* 225

tide (tīd): the rise and fall of the ocean's surface. *Brian
left his beach ball on the sand, but it floated out to sea
when the tide came in.* 322

toiling (toi′ liŋ): working hard to do something. *Glen was
toiling in the field all day.* 65

trench (trench): a ditch. *Craig dug a trench to drain the water away from the barn.* 163

trial (trī′ əl): a test. *The greenhouse owner gave Jonathan a trial job of watering plants.* 318

trilling (tri′ liŋ): singing with pleasantly trembling sounds. *Duane listened to the trilling sounds coming from the pond.* 11

trousers (traŭ′ zərz): pants. *The trousers were too large for Jeremiah.* 75

trudged (trəjd): walked in a tired way. *Chloe trudged up the hill with her arms full of groceries.* 76

unimportant (ən im pȯr′ tənt): not important. *Even though Karla thought fixing her bed was unimportant, she did it because her mother wanted her to.* 61

ungrateful (ən grāt′ fəl): not thankful. *People who are ungrateful are usually unhappy.* 26

urged (ərjd): strongly encouraged. *Grandma urged me to take several pieces of candy.* 93

vexed (vekst): troubled; upset. *Cameron was vexed that he missed the field trip.* 203

waddled (wä′ dəld): walked with short steps, swinging from side to side. *After spending the afternoon in the garden, the groundhog waddled back to its hole.* 18

Pronunciation Key
/a/ bat; /ā/ acorn; /är/ star; /e/ pet; /ē/ eagle; /er/ bear; /ər/ her; /i/ bit; /ī/ ivy; /ir/ deer; /ä/ top; /ō/ go; /ȯ/ lost; /ȯi/ coin; /aŭ/ out; /ȯr/ corn; /ə/ but; /ü/ boot; /yü/ use; /ù/ foot; /th/ thick; /th/ this; /ŋ/ bang; /zh/ measure

warehouse (wer' haủs) : a building where things to sell are stored. *Our new camera was shipped from the warehouse.* 110

warts (wȯrts) : small fleshy growths on the skin. *Elizabeth tried to get rid of the warts on her thumb.* 14

wealthy (wel' thē) : rich; having much money and many things. *The wealthy king planned a great feast.* 54

weary (wir' ē) : very tired. *John was weary after his day of preaching to the Jews.* 131

wick (wik) : the string that is burned in a candle. *Megan touched a burning match to the wick.* 143

widow (wi' dō) : a woman whose husband has died. *The widow made her living by baking bread to sell at the market.* 85

worthless (wərth' ləs) : having no value. *The vase was worthless after it was broken.* 161

wrath (rath) : anger. *Moses was not afraid of the king's wrath as he led the children of Israel out of Egypt.* 28

yelp (yelp) : a short, sharp bark. *Kenneth heard a yelp from the trapped dog.* 20

Acknowledgements

Artist: Charity Hoover and others

Cover Design: David Miller

Editorial committee: Ben Bergen, Keith E. Crider, James Hershberger, Sadie Schrock

"A Hero for Nero," adapted from "The Broken Vase," *Holmes Third Reader*. "A Hero for Nero," © 2000 Christian Light Publications, Inc., Harrisonburg, VA. All rights reserved.

"A Sledding Song," by Norman C. Schlichter.

"A Song for Twilight," by Nancy Byrd Turner, from *Beams of Light*.

"A Strange Visitor," adapted from "Indians for Thanksgiving," by Dorothy Heiderstadt, *Child Life*. © 1933 Rand McNally. All rights reserved. Adapted and reprinted by permission.

"A Strange Wall," author unknown.

"A Wooden God or the God of Heaven?" by Ruth K. Hobbs. © 2000 Christian Light Publications, Inc., Harrisonburg, VA. All rights reserved.

"Adventure After Dark," adapted from "The Pond at Night," *Neighbors on the Hill*, Second Reader. © 1943 Row Peterson.

"Adventures Down Under," adapted from "Danger and Adventure," from *Treats and Treasures*.

"Afternoon on a Hill," by Edna St. Vincent Millay.

"All About the Ocean," by Ruth K. Hobbs. © 2000 Christian Light Publications, Inc., Harrisonburg, VA. All rights reserved.

"At Dusk the Wild Creatures Move," by Jennifer Crider. © 2000 Jennifer Crider, Front Royal, VA. All rights reserved. Used by permission.

"At the Seaside," by Robert Louis Stevenson.

"Be Thou Removed," adapted from "Mountain Removed" in Light of Life. Reprinted by permission of Rod and Staff Publishers.

"Beaver Rescue," adapted from "Mickey the Beaver," by Kerry Wood, from *Up and Away*.

"Billfold Mystery," adapted from "Jem and the Billfold," *The Normal Third Reader*. "Billfold Mystery," © 2000 Christian Light Publications, Inc., Harrisonburg, VA. All rights reserved.

"Blind But Happy," by Fannie Crosby.

"Bread Through the Blizzard," adapted from "Daily Bread" by Bertha E. Bush, from *Beams of Light*. "Bread Through the Blizzard" © 2000 Christian Light Publications, Inc., Harrisonburg, VA. All rights reserved.

"Coals of Fire," adapted from *Holmes Third Reader*. Adaptation © 2000 Christian Light Publications, Inc., Harrisonburg, VA. All rights reserved.

"Come Back, Little Girl," Luke 8:41, 42, 49-56 KJV.

"Couldn't Aggravate Me!" adapted from *Holmes Third Reader*. Adaptation © 2000 Christian Light Publications, Inc., Harrisonburg, VA. All rights reserved.

"Danger in the Cornfield," adapted from "The Adventure in the Cornfield," by Jane Tompkins, from *The Raccoon Twins*, J. B. Lippincott.

"Do-As-You-Please Land," adapted from *Holmes Third Reader*. Adaptation © 2000 Christian Light Publications, Inc., Harrisonburg, VA. All rights reserved.

"Doors to Discovery," by Jennifer Crider. © 2000 Jennifer Crider, Front Royal, VA. All rights reserved. Used by permission.

386

"Dora Makes a Way," adapted from "Sally Finds a Way" from Looking Ahead from *Reading for Meaning*, by McKee, et al. Copyright © 1963 by Houghton Mifflin Company. Copyright renewed © 1991 by Beverly McKee Eaton, Paul E. Harrison, and Gloria Royer. Adapted by permission of Houghton Mifflin Company. All rights reserved.

"Exploring Guatemala," by Jennifer Crider. © 2000 Christian Light Publications, Inc., Harrisonburg, VA. All rights reserved.

"Finger Reading," adapted from "Louis Braille," by Bernice Frankel, *More Than Words*,

The McGraw-Hill Companies, Inc.

"God and Idols," Psalm 115:3-11, KJV.

"High Home in the Desert," adapted from "Blue Cornflower," by Ann Nolan Clark, from *Finding New Neighbors*.

"How Can Steam be Strong?" by Ruth K. Hobbs. © 2000 Christian Light Publications, Inc., Harrisonburg, VA. All rights reserved.

"How Do You Know It's Spring?" by Margaret Wise Brown.

"How Doth the Little Busy Bee," by Isaac Watts.

"How Tom Earned Miss Stubbs," adapted from "How Tom Earned His Calf," by Edward W. Frentz, from *Fact and Story Readers*, Book 3.

"I Cannot," adapted from "Faithful Shepherd Boy," *Holmes Third Reader*. "I Cannot," © 2000 Christian Light Publications, Inc., Harrisonburg, VA. All rights reserved.

"I Don't Care," adapted from *The Normal Third Reader*. Adaptation © 2000 Christian Light Publications, Inc., Harrisonburg, VA. All rights reserved.

"I Wish I Were a Rich Grown-Up," adapted from *The Normal Third Reader*. Adaptation © 2000 Christian Light Publications, Inc., Harrisonburg, VA. All rights reserved.

"I Won't Leave You," 2 Kings 2:1-12, KJV.

"If You Were," author unknown.

"Indian Children," by Annette Wynne.

"Is it a Ghost?" Mark 6:45-51, KJV.

"Little Fox, Man of the Family," adapted from "Little Fox of the Forest," by Katharine Keelor, from *Little Fox*, Macmillan.

"Long-Distance Healing," John 4:46-54, KJV.

"Look Out for the Blacksnakes," adapted from "Snake Story in a Story," Holmes Third Reader. Adaptation © 2000 Christian Light Publications, Inc., Harrisonburg, VA. All rights reserved.

"Luck or Blessing?" adapted from "The Stork's Nest," by Eleanor Hammond.

"Mighty Army of the Young," by John R. Colgan.

"My God Against Yours," 1 Kings 18:21-24, 28, 31-36, 38, 39, KJV

"My Quilt or Our House?" adapted from "Katy's Quilt," by Ruth Holbrook, from *Friends Far and Near*.

"One, Two, Three," by H. C. Bunner

"Polder Pals" by Jennifer Crider. © 2000 Christian Light Publications, Inc., Harrisonburg, VA.

All rights reserved.

"Produce Your Own," by Anna M. Pratt, from *Beams of Light*.

"Quarrel at the Ritter Place," by Ruth K. Hobbs. © 2000 Christian Light Publications, Inc., Harrisonburg, VA. All rights reserved.

"Ring Around the World," by Annette Wynne.

"Seagull," by Elizabeth Coatsworth.

"Snoopy Learns About Beeswax," by Ruth K. Hobbs. © 2000 Christian Light Publications, Inc., Harrisonburg, VA. All rights reserved.

"Thanksgiving Day," by Lydia Maria Child.